$\mathcal{M}$ORE THAN
PETTICOATS

—⟩•◦•⟨—

REMARKABLE
MINNESOTA
$\mathcal{W}$OMEN

D1114593

MORE THAN
PETTICOATS

———— ❦ ————

REMARKABLE
MINNESOTA
WOMEN

Bonnye E. Stuart

DISCARD

TWODOT®

GUILFORD, CONNECTICUT
HELENA, MONTANA
AN IMPRINT OF THE GLOBE PEQUOT PRESS

WEST BEND LIBRARY

DEDICATION

For my family, the Stuarts, the Butchers, the Perrets, the Hills,

you have provided the colors of my own story.

A · TWODOT® · BOOK

Copyright © 2004 by The Globe Pequot Press

All rights reserved. No part of this book may be reproduced or transmitted in any form by any means, electronic or mechanical, including photocopying and recording, or by any information storage and retrieval system, except as may be expressly permitted by the 1976 Copyright Act or by the publisher. Requests for permission should be made in writing to The Globe Pequot Press, P.O. Box 480, Guilford, Connecticut 06437.

TwoDot is a registered trademark of The Globe Pequot Press.

Cover photo: Women swimming at Lake Minnetonka. Courtesy of the Minnesota Historical Society.

Library of Congress Cataloging-in-Publication Data
Stuart, Bonnye.
    More than petticoats. Remarkable Minnesota women / Bonnye Stuart.— 1st. ed.
        p. cm. — (More than petticoats series)
    Includes bibliographical references and index.
    ISBN 0-7627-2357-2
        1. Women—Minnesota—Biography. 2. Women—Minnesota—History. 3.
Minnesota—Biography. I. Title: Remarkble Minnesota women. II. Title. III. Series.

CT3262.M6S78 2004
920.72'09776—dc22
[B]   2004052366

Manufactured in the United States of America
First Edition/First Printing

920.72
St9

CONTENTS

ᴀCKNOWLEDGMENTS

A book such as this is not the work of a single person but depends on the work of earlier researchers spanning many decades, even centuries. I have many people to recognize for their parts in my endeavor to get this manuscript completed.

First, I need to acknowledge the Minnesota Historical Society. The information I obtained from its rich resources was invaluable. I would also like to mention four universities with which I have been affiliated over the past few years and whose library resources provided much-needed material: St. Cloud State University in Minnesota; the University of West Florida in Pensacola, Florida; the University of North Carolina at Charlotte, North Carolina; and Winthrop University in Rock Hill, South Carolina.

I would also like to thank Lisa Heinrich not only for researching some of the featured women at the MNHS but, more importantly, for keeping me connected to my life in Minnesota after I moved away.

I would like to thank two organizations, the West Florida Literary Federation (WFLF) and the International Women's Writing Guild (IWWG). Neither probably knows how much it was a part of this project, but the commitment to fostering creativity and the encouragement to develop one's writing craft of both groups made me unwilling to let either of them down.

I would especially like to thank my best friend and collaborator, Gloria Stuart Butcher. She was my constant source of energy and inspiration to get the job done. Her pride in my work nourished not only my writing but also my soul.

Lastly, I would like to thank my devoted family. My children

Acknowledgments

David, Elizabeth, Jessica, and Christian; sons-in-law Frank and Jeff; and grandchildren Emily, Lauren, and Jack, all of whom provide the backdrop for all that I do. My husband, Laurence, deserves a very special mention. He has always allowed me the space to be exactly who I am. I am constantly replenished by his spirit and love. He has led me on a journey I never dreamed of, but I'm sure glad he did.

INTRODUCTION

Minnesota has a long and rich history that cannot be told without including the lives of the strong-willed and committed women who claim its heritage. The raw, frontier territory required stamina, intelligence, friendship and family values if they were to survive. But these women did more than merely survive; they helped bring Minnesota, powerful and enlightened, into the twenty-first century through their individual struggles against poverty, disease, oppression, and war. They were mothers and businesswomen, medical professionals and literary figures, political and religious leaders, and they all made the world a better place because of their accomplishments.

I could have written about one hundred women and still not have included all the important characters who left a positive mark on Minnesota's history. The women who are featured in this book are here by my choice. Their particular stories seemed inviting and interesting, and perhaps even personal. The writing of this book was an exciting adventure that brought my life full circle. Brought up by my mother in New Orleans and surrounded by a huge French family there, I experienced a colorful southern life. I learned the value of a close-knit family but also the acceptance of people who were different and unique. I didn't reconnect with my father until I was a mother myself. Born and reared in Wayzata, Minnesota, he began to share stories of his childhood. I found it hard to relate to his exciting tales of the frozen Mississippi River, the pleasure of sledding down snowy embankments, or the sound of lovesick loons calling their mates across one of Minnesota's 10,000 lakes. The images were just too far away from my world of sultry, humid nights and picnicking under moss-laden oaks in December. The Mississippi River in my part of the country rolled wide and lazy along the edge of the French Quarter as it headed out to the grassy marshes of the tepid Gulf of Mexico. Even visits to my aging grandmother and my aunt who practiced optometry in Minneapolis did not make me feel as if I belonged to that city. But, as fate would have it, I soon found myself teaching at St. Cloud State University, just north of Minneapolis. My father took me on a nostalgic tour of his Minneapolis and I connected with a cousin in Anoka. The Minnesota landscape was finally beginning to feel familiar.

Researching the women in this book opened a world I would never have known. I began to read about the Sioux and Fort Snelling, the beginnings of frontier towns and cities and the remarkable women who helped establish them. I read of suffragettes, writers, and actresses, all of whom demonstrated an indomitable spirit rooted in true midwestern values. As I read histories of the state and placed my heroines on their pedestals, I suddenly began to feel as if their stories were somehow a part of my own past.

I am proud that these strong and courageous women serve as a link to my own Minnesota heritage. I hope you find them remarkable as well.

JANE GREY SWISSHELM

1815–1884

Crusading Journalist

*J*ane stood on the high grassy bank of the Mississippi River looking down at the awful wreckage of her beloved printing press as it sunk beneath the waters. She had been editor of the *St. Cloud Visiter* for only a year and yet had managed to make many enemies. This malicious act, carried out under the thin veil of an August evening, was meant to silence her radical ideas about abolition and the equality of women. The perpetrators had hoped to run her out of business and out of Minnesota. As Jane stood evaluating her loss and determining her future, she thought back over her life and her commitment to freedom of speech and the quality of all Americans. Jane was determined that the loss of her expensive equipment would not deter her from her mission. She would not be silenced. She turned, not in anger, but in resolution. She would persevere in her mission.

Jane Grey Cannon was born on December 6, 1815, near Pittsburgh, Pennsylvania. Her family adhered to the strict teachings of the Covenanter faith, a branch of the European Presbyterian

EUGENE HILL, MINNESOTA HISTORICAL SOCIETY

Jane Grey Swisshelm

Church that allowed for no deviation from the rules, even though those rules were being tested and changed as immigrants adapted to a new life in America.

Tragedy struck when Jane's father died and left the family nearly penniless. Jane, only eight years old, and her brother, William, were put out to work until their mother could manage to save the house and reopen a village store. Jane worked by teaching lace making, and she took up painting on velvet, hoping to sell her creations. Once the family finances were in a respectable order, young Jane was sent to a boarding school, where she contracted the dreaded disease tuberculosis. This horrible scourge had already claimed the lives of her father and four other siblings. Jane's mother immediately pulled her out of school, hoping to keep alive the two daughters and one son she had left.

By the time Jane was fifteen, she had been teaching school for a year in her hometown and had already shown signs of rebellion. She abolished corporal punishment in her classroom and spoke out against her church for disallowing dancing but turning a blind eye to what was euphemistically called "stepping without music," as well as kissing at social gatherings, that posed as quilting bees. She particularly abhorred the Covenanters doctrine of damnation. She said, "I could not stay in heaven and know that anyone was enduring endless torments in some other place. I must go to their relief." Much of her exasperation was aimed at the injustice of her brother's being damned for not following the authority of the church, moving west rather than becoming a cabinetmaker's apprentice as his church recommended. No one could have predicted at this time the prominent role this thin, small woman with a pleasant face would play in the early history of Minnesota or the national recognition she would achieve as she joined the cause for equal rights, both of slaves and women. Jane had taken to heart the Biblical message, "The tongue is a powerful weapon. Words slay men."

In 1836 Jane married James Swisshelm, the son of a farmer and a possessive mother. The Swisshelms sought to convert Jane to the Methodist Church, but she steadfastly held onto her own religious beliefs. Unable to exact her conversion, James—with his mother's approval—insisted that Jane give up her painting as proof of her wifely obedience. Jane acquiesced as she was excitedly looking forward to a move to Louisville, Kentucky, where James was to go into a trading business with his brother Samuel. Jane was hoping that things would improve for her marriage. They did not; if anything, matters got worse. Soon the brothers took to arguing and the business began to falter. But Jane found the conservative culture of the South much more troubling than her husband's business woes. She reviled the conditions of women and slaves. In her writings she described men who crowded the city ready to "insult every woman who ventured on the street without a male protector, by a stare so lascivious as could not be imagined on the American free soil." She described the women there as "captive female flesh abused by lash and libido."

As bad as the conditions for women were, Jane could not even put into words the deplorable conditions the slaves suffered at the hands of their owners: "There in Louisville we gained our ideas of slaveholders, and found the utter impotence of language to convey any impression of them." Jane couldn't stand the inhumane treatment of slaves, and it wasn't long before she let her feelings be known. She befriended a black family and worked to open a school to teach their children. Because of violent threats against her enterprise, the school closed after only one day.

When the dueling brothers finally split, James started his own carriage business, and Jane began working as a corsetmaker. Her business was very successful, and as it flourished, she began to hire on seamstresses to help with some of the work. James, however, was less than successful. His carriage business began to fail, and he could not handle his wife's success, which he saw as an insult to his masculinity. Jane wrote, "I worked until I was tired, thinking of all the sacrifices I had made to be my husband's housekeeper and keep myself in a woman's sphere, and here was the outcome! I was degrading him from his position as breadwinner."

In the summer of 1839, Jane received the sad news that her mother was dying of cancer. She wanted to go home immediately to tend to her. But James wanted her to stay in Louisville and quoted scripture that a woman must obey her husband. Jane chose to leave. After her mother's death, James, ever anxious to control his wife and improve his finances, decided to sue the estate of Jane's mother for "covertures"—the right of a husband to take a wife's wages and fees. James asserted that although Jane had not received any money for taking care of her mother, she should have, and he was thus entitled to that money from the estate. In 1842, desperate to stop this legal action, Jane agreed to join her husband, who by this time had left Louisville and returned to live with his mother on the family farm in Pennsylvania.

It was in this unhappy situation that Jane began her career as a journalist. Writing under the pseudonym "Jennie Deans," Jane's poems, stories, and rhymes were published in two Philadelphia newspapers, but the world was not yet to glimpse the force of Jane's invectives, nor the stance she would ultimately take against a society that appeared to her more and more unjust.

It wasn't long before James again threatened Jane with legal action. This time he refused to sign a paper that would allow some of Jane's mother's property to be sold. According to the law, the husbands of her two daughters had control over her property. Jane's sister Elizabeth's husband had agreed to sign, but James would not. Jane took a bold action. She began to study law. She read the law books of family friend Samuel Black and began her investigation into property rights for women. Edward Stanton, a bright young attorney with an interest in changing some of the antiquated laws (later to be secretary of war), helped Jane win her eventual court victory. Her case, *Swisshelm v. Swisshelm* became one of the most important legal landmarks of the nineteenth century. In its decision the Pennsylvania Supreme Court accused James of trying to strip Jane of her right to her mother's property.

It was about this time that Jane began writing her *Spirit of Liberty* articles for the Liberty party newspaper. In them she focused on married women's relationships with their husbands, discussing property rights, oppression, and the right to education. Her first articles were signed only with her initials, and that the author was a woman was not even suggested. By 1845 Jane, referring to herself, as a political journalist, as she noted in her autobiography *A Half Century*, had completed the transition from "anonymous publicist to outspoken advocate of women's rights." She began to sign her full name to her articles that appeared in the abolitionist newspaper the *Pittsburgh Commercial Journal.*

Because many of those who wanted to abolish slavery did not necessarily want women to gain additional rights, Jane was forced to abandon writing for the *Journal.* Undaunted, she launched her own newspaper, the *Pittsburgh Saturday Visiter* (as she spelled it), a small four-page weekly that served as both an anti-slavery platform and a vehicle for women's rights. With her first issue in December 1847, Jane became the first woman in the United States to own and edit a political newspaper, and she did so nearly six months before the now famous Seneca Falls Convention would make history with its Declaration of Principles for the national women's rights movement. Jane had complete control of her paper and was now not only a reformer and a dissenter with a voice but one with a newspaper through which to disseminate those opinions. She edited the *Saturday Visiter* for five years, and when subscription figures topped out at 6,000 the *Visiter* took its place as one of the most widely read reform newspapers in the country.

Family problems again changed Jane's personal and career paths. The birth of her only daughter and quarrels with her husband forced Jane to sell her newspaper, though she continued to write articles and essays for publication. When she could no longer stand her husband's directives and cruel behavior, Jane made the decision to move to Saint Cloud, Minnesota, one of the small, bustling settlements on the edge of the frontier, about one hundred miles north of Saint Paul. Farmers here went about their chores with a stoic spirit, while townspeople grappled with the growing pains of a thriving river community. The race for land, Indian trade opportunities, and timber and railroad charters was on, and the Minnesota population had nearly quintupled in size in just three years, from 32,000 people in 1854 to 150,000 in 1857. Life was tough and hardships were expected. The promise of a better way of life always loomed in the future, but few saw those good times. Wave after wave of disease stormed through the sleepy countryside—tuberculosis, scarlet fever, cholera, diphtheria, and whooping cough descended upon the new settlers, at times threatening to wipe out not just entire families but whole towns as well.

The horrific locust infestation of 1856 devastated the corn and other crops growing in the Minnesota sun, including below-the-ground crops like potatoes and carrots. And when the hungry pests were finished with the crops, they ravaged home gardens and wild flowers, leaving the area desolate. Bears, wolves, and other native animals were constant threats to family safety. Local Indians were also to be watched warily.

But pestilence, plague, and wild animals seemed more palatable to Jane than living in Philadelphia with her husband and his domineering mother. In 1857, when Jane took her young daughter and left James, she uttered the parting words, "After fifteen years in his mother's house I must run away or die."

Jane knew of the dire conditions on the Minnesota frontier from the letters of her sister, Elizabeth Cannon Mitchell, who was living there with her five children and a sixth on the way. Her husband, Henry Mitchell, had ventured into the territory looking for a place with good business prospects.

Once in Minnesota, Jane planned to leave all the emotional family battles behind her and live in a small cabin on a quiet lake some 12 miles from the city. She hoped she could also escape the pervasive inequality of women she had fought against for so long, "the irrepressible conflict . . . thinking I should see no more of our national curse." But that was not to be. In Minnesota, women, though working farms and tending crops, were still second-class citizens.

When Jane arrived in Saint Cloud, her national reputation came with her. Her past successes included forcing U.S. senators to give in to her demands to open the reporters' section of the Senate Gallery to women and having her correspondence solicited for publication by Horace Greeley's *Tribune*, one of the most powerful newspapers in the country. All that was behind her now, and she looked forward to a tranquil life in Minnesota. But even before her arrival, her family had convinced her it would not be safe to live outside the city on the lake she had pictured in her dreams. Instead, Jane and her six-year-old daughter, Zo, moved into her sister's home in town.

Typically, the women of the area were strong, of German stock, and involved in the hard work of daily farm chores. Wives faced the constant peril of childbirth and stress of child rearing. By contrast Jane had the small, slight build of Scottish gentry and had arrived in Saint Cloud without a husband. She threw herself into the major political issues of the day, an exclusively male domain, and not only made her own opinions known but also had the audacity to question and criticize her male counterparts.

Jane soon came to the attention of George Brott, a business acquaintance of her brother-in-law, who had started a newspaper, the *Minnesota Advertiser,* as a way to advertise his real estate business. He had given little time to the running of the paper, and now it was in financial trouble. He needed the paper as a vehicle for his real estate ads and didn't want to see it fold. Brott offered to sell Jane the newspaper. She resisted at first, but then he sweetened the deal by throwing in some real estate, corner lots that were not saleable to the public. Jane gave in but warned Brott that, "my normal state is mutual antagonism to the superior sex; and contempt for their affectation for their superiority."

During that first summer and fall, Jane, though busy with her own journalistic activities, observed Saint Cloud society and its goings-on. Riverboats cruised the Mississippi River and upon their broad, flat decks lively bands played as highbrow citizens danced the night away. Fireworks adorned the dark skies, and festive music and laughter floated out over the dark waters. Jane saw an exclusive world, one reserved for the "old" proprietors. Newcomers were not welcomed.

She found the history of her new town very troubling. Saint Cloud was a city founded and settled in three distinct areas, not only geographically, but politically as well: Uppertown, Middletown, and Lowertown. Middletown was inhabited by mostly thrifty, stoic German Catholics. As Democrats they were controlled by Sylvanus Lowry, a despotic politician and figurehead of "slave power" in the Minnesota territory. Lowry was a proslavery Democrat from Virginia who had owned slaves there and had brought some of them with him to Minnesota. He maintained proslavery contacts in Kentucky and Tennessee and encouraged like-minded people to settle in Uppertown. His was the circle that entertained on the lavish riverboats that trolled the Mississippi.

Jane had met the overbearing Lowry on her stagecoach trip west. These two strong personalities seemed fated to clash. The farmers of Middletown needed Uppertown's professional elite of bankers and lawyers. Uppertown's elite, in turn, needed Middletown's farmers and workers as clients. Lowertown's settlers were newer to the area, mainly from New England and the Middle Atlantic states. They were mostly Protestants and were viewed as competitors for the available farmland. Lowertown became the common enemy of the folks of Middletown and Uppertown.

It was in Lowertown that Henry Mitchell had scouted his business opportunities, and it was here that Jane and her family settled. With her acceptance of the editorship of Brott's *Advertiser,* Jane became an influential citizen of the city of Saint Cloud. She changed the name of her newspaper to the *St. Cloud Visiter* and on December 10, 1857, published the first issue. Across the front page ran a Jeffersonian credo affirming the equality of mankind.

That first winter Jane threw herself into her newspaper business. Despite the long hours and hard work, she couldn't help noticing that the river parties had moved inside, from the river boats to the warm, luxurious homes of the socially prominent. There were dinners and card parties, and the spirited music and conversations could be heard in the streets of town. Lowry, ever in charge, invited only members of the old families. Jane, even though she could now boast the proprietorship of the newspaper and ownership of the corner lots, would never be included in Lowry's prestigious elite. Lowry and his group flaunted the fact that they were running the city.

By February 18, 1858, Jane could contain her views no longer and ran articles lambasting Lowry for his slavery connections. She wrote a front page editorial saying that a vote for the Democratic ticket meant a vote for "a pair of handcuffs." Lowry was infuriated. He publicly attacked Jane, painting her as a woman who had been abandoned by her husband. He accused her of being unsexed and an aberration of nature. Jane felt she had no choice but to pull out her big guns, so to speak, and point them directly at Lowry and his inner circle. Jane began to help Republican Party organizers, and Lowry became their primary target. As the assaults continued, Lowry convinced a prominent citizen of Uppertown, fellow Democrat James Shepley, to give a speech denigrating Jane and women like her whom they felt did not fit into the traditional role of mother and homemaker.

Though gender roles on the frontier were less rigid than they were in the more civilized east, women were still expected to remain within the boundaries set for them by the menfolk. Jane fought back against the Shepley speech, writing that the worst type of woman is not one who is independent and strong willed but rather one who thinks she is superior to all others merely because she has married status and wealth. It was an editorial that described many of the upper-crust wives.

In retaliation Lowry and others raided the offices of the *Visiter* and threw pieces of the press into the Mississippi River. They left behind a note: "St. Cloud, March 24, 1858 —Editor of the *Visiter*: The citizens of St. Cloud have determined to abate the nuisance of which you have made the *Visiter* a striking specimen. They have decided that it is fit only for the inmates of brothels, and you seem to have some experience of the tastes of such persons. You will never have the opportunity to repeat the offense in this town, without paying a more serious penalty than you do now. By order of the Commander of Vigilance."

Jane was not afraid. Despite ominous warnings "that she be murdered or assaulted, or set adrift on the Mississippi River with her hands tied behind her back," Jane attended a meeting protesting the dismantling of her press. Expecting serious trouble, she made out her will and took along a bodyguard to whom she had given the instruction to shoot her should she be taken into the hands of the mob. Jane needn't have worried. The townspeople stood behind her and defended not only her right to free speech but theirs as well. At the meeting two committees were formed to deal with the issues at hand. One would draft a resolution protesting the destruction of the newspaper. The other committee was mandated to find a way to rebuild and refurnish the newsroom and its equipment. Twenty-eight investors formed the Printing Company of Saint Cloud, and soon the newspaper's press was up and running again.

The community had united against a political foe, and it was reported "that without regard to party, they fought the issue through to victory." As soon as the press was working again, Jane reprinted her scathing review of Shepley's "Categories of Women" speech. Still searching for a way to silence the errant newspaper editor, Shepley brought a libel suit against the twenty-eight investors, now owners of the press. Their livelihoods were on the line, and Jane did not want to hurt the very men who had supported her. To prevent the libel suit from going to court, Jane agreed to print a retraction and never attack Lowry or his cronies again in the *Visiter*. The opposition accepted her terms and dropped the suit.

But Jane was not so easily defeated. After printing the retraction she had promised, she shut down the *Visiter* offices, ensuring, as she had agreed, that the paper would never again print anything opposed to Lowry's politics.

The next day, Jane started a new newspaper, the *St. Cloud Democrat*, and the first article she published was the infamous reprint reviewing Shepley's "Categories of Women" speech. It seemed this woman had indeed beaten the entrenched system. Jane was never again threatened with losing her newspaper for what she published.

By 1860 Jane was one of Saint Cloud's most important citizens. She held bimonthly receptions for important Republican celebrities, including Governor Ramsey and Lieutenant Governor Donnelly. She spent much of her time traveling around the state giving lectures on a variety of subjects, from abolition to suffrage. She spoke out about integrity and equality.

Jane had fought against slavery and had championed women's rights. She had been in complete control of her newspapers, and her mission to integrate her beliefs and values into the news of the day meant that her work became not only history but her personal story as well.

Not long after watching her press sink into the Mississippi, Jane became a Washington, D.C., correspondent for the *New York Tribune.* She interviewed President Abraham Lincoln, befriended Mary Todd Lincoln, and established herself as one of the best-known journalists of her time. The fact that Jane Swisshelm could neither vote nor hold office did not keep this determined woman from becoming an important politician. In 1860 she spoke in the Hall of Representatives in Saint Paul, and in 1862 she spoke in the Senate on women's legal disabilities.

In 1863 Jane sold her Saint Cloud newspaper to her nephew, William Mitchell. Today it is called the *St. Cloud Times.*

In her later life Jane involved herself in hospital work, helping to nurse the wounded of the Civil War. In 1865 she started yet another newspaper, the *Reconstructionist,* and, defying protests by the printer's union, she employed women as type compositors. Her newspaper office was twice set on fire in retaliation.

In her cancer-ridden old age, Jane Grey Cannon Swisshelm lay on her bed surrounded by her loved ones. Her sister, Elizabeth, who had seen Jane through the tumultuous years in Saint Cloud and who had applauded her sister when she was honored as the

Mother of the Republican Party in Minnesota, was there. Her daughter, Zo, had traveled from Chicago to be by her mother's side. And, thankfully, there was another person present, a newspaperman sent from his paper in Pittsburgh to record the dying words of a great journalist, for it seems that Jane had burned all her personal papers except three short stories; one letter to an old friend, George W. Julian, an abolitionist and vice-presidential candidate on the Free Soil ticket of 1852; and her 1880 autobiography, *A Half Century*. Besides these writings, Jane Swisshelm would be known to future generations only through her newspaper articles and her passionate editorials. Jane died on July 22, 1884. Pieces of her beloved press still remain beneath the muddy waters of the Mississippi River in Saint Cloud, Minnesota, marked by a distinguished plaque placed near the bridge leading to St. Cloud State University, where today men and women study and learn the skills of news reporting in a state-of-the art, nationally accredited Department of Mass Communications. Jane Swisshelm would be proud.

HARRIET BISHOP
1817–1883

Pioneer Educator

*H*arriet lifted her tired body from the rough blanket where she rested in the shade of the tree-lined river. She was still recovering from her seasickness on the long voyage up the Mississippi River when she felt a rising tide of homesickness wash over her. Had it been prudent to leave the civilized cradle of New England, where her family protected and cherished her? Only time would tell, she reckoned, as she climbed the steep bank to get a good look at the town that had just recently changed its name from "Pig's Eye" to Saint Paul, a place to which God had "called" her. The town before her was nothing more than a crude river port of meager housing and rough characters. It was set alongside a deep channel in the river, the last upstream spot for boat traffic. Just ahead lay miles of dangerous rapids, steep cliffs, and the roiling Falls of Saint Anthony. She saw that there was indeed much work to be done. "Here was a field to be cultivated, a garden of untrained flowers to be tended," she said, ready now to begin her mission.

Harriet Bishop was born on January 1, 1817, in Panton, a small sleepy town on the western edge of Vermont, the first English

Engraved by J.C.Buttre

Harriet E Bishop

MINNESOTA HISTORICAL SOCIETY

Harriet Bishop

settlement in Addison County. Harriet was the third daughter of Putnam and Miranda Bishop, and at an early age she exhibited signs of growing into a devoutly religious child. Harriet read her Bible earnestly, taking to heart all its tenets, and when she turned thirteen, Harriet committed herself to God by being baptized in the cold waters of Lake Champlain. She felt privileged to be recognized as the youngest active member of her Baptist church, a religious affiliation she was to keep dear to her heart throughout her long life. The farming town of her birth boasted of hosting Benjamin Franklin in 1776, while he was on his way north to enlist Canada's help in the American Revolution. Panton's citizens also told stories of Benedict Arnold and his defeat by the British Navy on nearby Lake Champlain, giving a name to the local landmark, Arnold Bay, where some of his ships had run aground. But Harriet, an avid reader, was more interested in stories of strong women with a sense of duty and purpose. She pored through the memoirs of missionaries like Harriet Newall and Anna Hudson and read about their trials and tribulations trying to convert "the heathen" of Burma. She was determined that she, too, would dedicate herself to teaching and converting lost souls.

Her first move away from her loving home and family in Panton was to the Fort Edwards Institute in New York to earn her teaching credentials. Soon after that she began to teach in the Essex County, New York, public school system. But after ten years Harriet felt she had somewhere else to go, something else to do. Wanting to move westward where she felt there was a greater opportunity to make a difference in the world, she enrolled in the Catharine Beecher teacher-training course in Albany, New York. At this time there was a shortage of pioneer teachers, and Beecher had convinced William Slade, former governor of Vermont, to establish the National Board of Popular Education. After training the students in frontier-adapting skills, Beecher would place the teachers in various positions of need, far from the homes they knew, in the uncivilized territories of a growing nation.

Harriet was one of the first thirty-five recruits at Beecher's school and considered herself fortunate to be in training for a teaching position out west. She immersed herself in her studies, learning how to deal with the difficulties that might arise on the lonely frontier, from health dangers to shortages of school supplies to lack of spiritual training among children and adults alike. And when a fortuitous letter arrived from Thomas Williamson of Minnesota desperately seeking a teacher for the children of Saint Paul, a woman who "should love the Savior and for his sake should be willing to forego, not only many of the religious privileges and elegances of New England towns, but some of neatness also," she was ready to answer the call. Harriet converted the doubts of friends and family into strong incentives to follow her dream and later wrote about the simple river town, "I was more needed here than at any other spot on earth." In the years between 1847 and 1850, the organization known as the National Board of Popular Education would send out more than 400 teachers to schools from Ohio to California. Harriet was not only a member of the original Beecher training class, she was also the first graduate to be sent out to educate the children of the frontier.

Harriet first stepped foot on Minnesota territory at a small Dakota Indian river landing on the Mississippi called Kaposia. She had endured a long steamboat ride across Lake Erie, over the turbulent Ohio River, and up the stately Mississippi River. Here, in Little Crow's Dakota village, missionary Dr. Williamson, his sister Mary, and a band of local Indians met her. Little did she know at this time the part Chief Little Crow was to play in the future of Minnesota, the bloody massacre of 1862, and the ignominious fate of his beloved Indians. But, here, in the present, she could see there was much work to be done.

After a few days of rest, she was taken by canoe, 9 miles upriver to Saint Paul, a town of only a few homes and a handful of stores, inhabited by fifty settlers, twenty of whom were school-age children. She was also told to expect at her school some children of the "Friendlies," Indians aligned with the white man. She took a deep breath; this would be the home of her new school, the first school, besides the missions, in the entire territory of Minnesota.

Only days after her arrival in Minnesota, a land so different and foreign to the New England woman, Harriet stood proudly at the doorstep of her new school. Oh, she was not proud that the 10-foot by 12-foot classroom was housed in an old blacksmith's shop. She was not proud that its walls were mud-packed and caked with rotting bark. She was not proud that snakes and rats scurried to and from their homes long hidden in the decaying logs of the muddy hovel. But she was, oh, so proud of the ten children who attended that summer day, July 19, 1847, when she opened the doors of her school for the first time. She looked around at her students seated uncomfortably on the boards laid atop wooden pegs driven into the logs of the walls, then she trailed her eyes to the setting hen, still in attendance, who had refused to move from her nest in the former abandoned shop. She continued to scan the room; everything was the best she could make it. She smiled when her eyes rested on the rickety table in the center of the room where she would work; it would be her desk. Her students were descendants of French Canadians, English settlers, Scandinavian pioneers, African Americans, and Indian children of the Sioux, Dakota, and Chippewa, all of them sporting furtive faces, not sure where they were or why. Harriet took control of her charges and scrubbed each dirty face clean with a bar of soap before the day's lessons in English and French began.

Harriet loved the new scenes and smells of Saint Paul. The homes she passed along the river were meager log cabins, dugouts, and sod houses just barely able to be classified as permanent dwellings. Large brick homes on limestone foundations would come much later. This was civilization at its beginnings. The damp and dark cabins were outfitted with homemade furniture fashioned of split logs and leather strappings. A one-legged bedstead would be fitted tightly into a corner of the room and hitched to pegs in the two walls. Primitive trundle beds that could slide under the bigger bed during the day served as the children's sleeping quarters. The food available here was much different than back in Vermont. The Saint Paul market of 1850 sold buffalo tongue and venison, and the prices of this odd fare were quite dear. Families from the countryside would bring in sugar, flour, lard, cheese, molasses, and dried fruits to sell. The area may have offered few cultural and social amenities, but people rarely went hungry. Gala meals were offered for all sorts of celebrations, and successful scouts and bountiful frontiersmen often gave lavish feasts for the settlers to enjoy.

Though she was a dedicated teacher, Harriet felt she needed to do more than educate her students with book knowledge. She was filled with a missionary passion and a social reformer's zeal. She wanted to civilize her charges, bringing morality and order to their lives. She began modestly by decorating the small classroom with evergreen sprigs brought in from the woods beyond, but then almost immediately turned her efforts toward permanently improving the school's facilities. That first winter she began the Saint Paul Circle of Industry to help raise funds for a new school. She was so successful that the new school building was finished in 1848 and instantly became the center of activity in the town, serving as a voting room, courtroom, lecture hall, and church. Her school was thriving, and in just two years Harriet's student enrollment had grown to 150 children.

Harriet was committed just as strongly to her religious avocation as she was to teaching, and she felt that the students should not be instructed just to read and write but, as she stated herself, "also be taught the Word of God." Just two weeks after establishing her small school, Harriet began a Sunday worship service there. It was the first in town, and the only Baptist church north of Iowa and west of the Mississippi River. As she was the sole Baptist in the area, she welcomed all citizens to her congregation, setting up separate classes for Methodists and Presbyterians. Her efforts resulted in the establishment of the First Baptist Church of Saint Paul on July 25, 1847, a church still prominent in the city today, 150 years later. The congregation grew steadily, and Harriet realized she needed some help. Relief came in the form of Deacon Abram Cavender, a blacksmith who settled in Saint Paul and began working to help Harriet with some of the church duties. Still lacking a permanent minister for the flock, Harriet wrote numerous petitions to the Baptist Home Missions Society Board for a candidate. The board responded by sending Reverend John P. Parsons, an energetic man who set about formally organizing the church. Harriet was overjoyed to see work begin on the erection of a small church on an elevated plot that became known as Baptist Hill. But an unpredictable tragedy was to strike the fledging church. Returning from a trip east to procure funding, Reverend Parsons was murdered and robbed of the money he had collected. It was a sad sight and many tears were shed as, ironically, the first service held in the newly built church was the funeral of Reverend Parsons. But the church succeeded beyond Harriet's wildest dreams, and it remained dedicated to helping people of all faiths. She called First Baptist a "religious Forwarding House" because it had played a part in the foundation of many churches of various denominations throughout the city.

Harriet was also in love. She had been described as attractive with a good figure and expressive eyes, and she rationalized that this was why she had attracted the attention of the promising young lawyer eight years her junior. James K. Humphrey was from a good family, and the two were deeply committed to each other. They became engaged and a fall wedding was planned. James built a honeymoon cottage for Harriet on beautiful Ryan Avenue. Harriet imagined sitting with her husband around the cozy fire in the Early Victorian-style home, with its limestone foundation and gabled roof, as the brisk fall air turned to winter cold. But it was not to be. James's sister did not approve of his choice for a wife. She said that Harriet was too old for her brother and forbade the marriage. Harriet was devastated. She had loved James deeply, but it seemed he did not love her enough to go against his sister's wishes. The wedding was called off, and James sold the lovely house that was to be their home. By November 1850 Harriet was still overcome with sorrow and disappointment. In an effort to heal her broken heart, she left Minnesota and put all the memories of her fiancé behind her. After months of recuperation, Harriet returned to Saint Paul and was ready to get back to work.

She turned her attentions from teaching to social reform. She took up the battle against alcohol and spoke out often on eliminating the sale and use of "devil water." She was one of the driving forces behind establishing the Sons of Temperance in the spring of 1849. Temperance soon became a political issue and remained a cause of Harriet's throughout her life. She felt so compelled by the issue that she wrote a book of poetry, *Minnesota Then and Now*, with temperance as the foundation of her good versus evil theme. She opened a "Female Seminary" to serve the poor in 1850 and made sure all her residents signed the pledge of abstinence promulgated by the Sons of Temperance.

But that life was soon put aside when the first alarm of the Civil War was sounded and the battle for the nation's very existence posed more immediate problems. The country was divided and Minnesota joined in the fight. Harriet had fallen in love again, and this time the marriage ceremony went ahead, though perhaps it shouldn't have. Harriet married John McConkey, a harness maker and widower with four young children. Harriet lovingly cared for the children on her own while John fought in the Civil War with the First Minnesota Regiment. But all was not well. John was discharged from his service for medical reasons, but what was worse, he returned to Harriet and the children with a serious drinking problem. Harriet, a woman with definite ideas of temperance and equality of women, was perhaps too much for McConkey, who continued to drink and treat his wife unfairly. The unhappy marriage was dissolved nine years later. Harriet, in a bold move for her gender and time, reclaimed her maiden name and was known from then on as Mrs. Harriet Bishop.

By 1867 Harriet was once again a single woman, but more importantly, she was a respected leader in the community. Her heart, though hurt and battered, was still set on helping those who could not help themselves. She was determined, persistent, and focused on her commitments to God and humankind. She often antagonized those who stood in her way, but she felt it her calling to forge ahead, providing humanitarian services to a now bustling city of industry and commerce.

Saint Paul had grown by leaps and bounds since 1847. More than twenty steamboats a day were docking at the two landings around which the town had grown. The increase in river trade brought other industries. The carriage and cart trade flourished, restaurants and inns sprang up to feed and house the workers, and livestock ran through the streets where businesspeople hustled to get their jobs done. It was during this time that Harriet finished her book, *Floral Home: Or, First Years of Minnesota*, which invited settlers to Minnesota and extolled the virtues of the state, calling the climate one of its greatest attributes. But during the cold, frigid winter months, most activity came to a standstill. The river would freeze over, preventing all boats from entering the port. Saint Paul, now used to the busy days of trade and commerce, sought a connection to the rest of the country by railroad, the Iron Horse of the West.

A plan was set—in 1856 Congress granted land for four railroads that were to emanate from Saint Paul. After a few setbacks due to political graft and various troubles, the rails were laid. There was an immediate growth spurt as settlements sprung up, lining the iron tracks with homes and businesses. The Northern Pacific ran westward and was a significant contributor to the expansion of markets for the Minnesota lumber trade. James J. Hill completed the Great Northern line through North Dakota and Montana and reached Pacific Coast markets in 1893.

The railroads were changing the face of the city as well. Stately homes were springing up to accommodate the families of emerging entrepreneurs and railroad barons. Huge Victorian villas built from area limestone quarries graced tree-lined Summit Avenue. A fellow Vermonter built a Summit beauty of gray limestone in 1862, and the rooms were said to be furnished with the finest French and Italian imports. River trade and a stagecoach line had made its owner, James Burbank, rich. It was these wealthy people that Harriet sought out for donations to help the poor immigrants pouring into the city to work the mills and build the railroad lines. Some had become wealthy, but so many more were needy.

She organized the Ladies Christian Union specifically to help the less fortunate of the community. In 1867 these women successfully purchased a home in Lowertown to tend to those who were homeless or destitute. The Home for the Friendless is still in existence today as the Wilder Residence East, a place of care for the elderly.

By 1877 Harriet had changed her role once again. She moved away from teaching and secular duties, listing her occupation as author and lecturer in the city directory. She was appointed by the Minnesota Woman's Christian Temperance Union to travel through the state to lecture and help organize new chapters of the organization. She became a driving force and charter member of the establishment of the Minnesota Woman Suffrage Association in 1881. Though Harriet had been schooled in the Catharine Beecher tradition that held that women were important in the domestic sphere as molders of character and moral gatekeepers of a community, she believed they were capable of much more. This was an issue of great importance to Harriet, and she had fought quietly for women's rights all her life. By this time Sojourner Truth had delivered her famous "Ain't I a Woman?" speech; Harriet Beecher Stowe, sister of Catharine Beecher who had sent Harriet out to teach the children of Saint Paul, had written *Uncle Tom's Cabin*; and Elizabeth Cady Stanton and Susan B. Anthony had established the American Equal Rights Association. Harriet was proud to be a woman fighting for equality. She wrote in her book *Floral Home*, "I have never so felt my soul grow with enthusiasm, the fact that I am an American woman."

Harriet's Saint Paul Circle of Industry, a group of eight women, raised the necessary monies to build a new school. She formed the Baptist Sewing Circle to provide funds for the church's expenses and to pay off the mortgage on the new church building. She was an avid volunteer and held a number of executive positions in the community. She was an active member of Saint Paul's literary circle. Besides her Minnesota history book, she wrote *Dakota War Whoop: Or Indian Massacres and War in Minnesota of 1862–63* which examined Indian and settler relationships. In 1857 she served as president of the Philecelesian, the newly formed literary club. In 1880 Harriet finished a beautiful handwritten account of her church, *History of the First Baptist Church of St. Paul.*

Harriet died in August 1883 in Saint Paul of "general asthenia." She was only sixty-six years old, but she had seen her world change many times over. She had started off amid the well-manicured farms of Vermont and had traversed the country, where she had seen the landscape change to the rough backwoods of Minnesota. She had seen a dirty shanty town grow into marble-domed capital city, and she had seen a one-room schoolhouse expand into statewide educational facilities. She had been a part of it all. She had fought long and hard for human rights, and her legacy would live on. Her first school house in the blacksmith's shop overlooked what was to become Harriet Island—a park area for picnics, festivals, and fairs, donated to the city in her memory by Dr. Justus Ohage Sr., a Saint Paul physician who fought in the Civil War and performed the first successful gall bladder operation in the nation in 1886. The *Harriet Bishop* cruise ship, named to honor Minnesota's first schoolteacher, operates out of Harriet Island. An elementary school in Rochester has been named after the pioneer educator. The First Baptist Church, still community-centered, cherishes Harriet's handwritten history, and the Minnesota Historical Society celebrates Harriet Bishop and her accomplishments in its *Minnesota A to Z* exhibit in the history center.

Harriet never regretted leaving her comfortable life in New England and felt she had ultimately led a better life because of that decision. She wrote, "No where is there a more favorable field for the cultivation of a spirit to be useful, and to accommodate oneself to circumstances, than upon the frontier of a new and sparsely populated region." For Harriet Bishop that special spot became her final resting place: She was buried in Saint Paul's Oakland Cemetery.

Martha Ripley
1843–1912

Prairie Physician

*T*he tired and bedraggled girl could stop searching. She had finally found the house, sitting serenely atop a small turf mound in a quiet Minneapolis neighborhood. It had been an arduous journey for her, and suddenly she felt very weary. Though it was not a fancy place, and its welcoming front porch was a little too narrow, the girl saw in this unassuming residence her only salvation. She looked up one more time at the plaque nailed to the low over-hanging roof and then laboriously mounted the wooden steps, heavy with her burden. A pleasant-looking woman opened the front door and, knowing immediately why the girl was here, bade her to come inside. Putting a friendly and consoling arm around the girl's shoulders, the older woman led her through the entryway and into the parlor. The girl sat down, sobbing. Amid tears streaking down her trip-worn face, she began to tell her sad story. The matron grabbed a handkerchief and placed it in the girl's hand; then she, too, sat down and listened. She knew it would be a long story.

The girl explained that she had lived her entire life in a small town not too far away and had been engaged for a while to a

MINNESOTA HISTORICAL SOCIETY

Martha Ripley

respectable man who was much older than she. He had seemed true and honest, and she had been very much in love. When she discovered she was pregnant, the man had vowed to stick by her and protect her. He had given her a little money and sent her off to the big city to begin a new life for the two of them, away from the wagging tongues in their hometown, a familiar but unforgiving place. There in the city, no one would know their wedding date or the number of months between their marriage and child's birth. He would join her very soon. The expectant mother had waited patiently, but the man had postponed his trip to be with her again and again, saying that he "could not come just yet." Then, one day, frantic and hopelessly in debt, she called home to talk to her lover. To her shock she learned that the man had moved to a distant city and had no intention of making good on his promise of marriage.

Now, nearing her due date, the girl was desperate. She had heard about the kind works of Dr. Ripley and the Maternity Hospital, and she was hoping to plead her case before the good doctor. Childbirth was dangerous for women in the 1880s. Many expected to die and often wrote good-bye letters to their loved ones before their delivery time. Others shared with their diaries their deep fear of dying while giving birth or, at best, suffering excruciating pain during the ordeal. If they were lucky enough to live, many women faced years of pain and suffering from tearing, infection, or other complications. The girl had heard that space was limited and beds scarce at the Maternity Hospital, but this was the only medical institution in the area that would admit unwed mothers.

As the desolate mother-to-be hung her head in shame, the older woman held her tightly to her chest. The girl repeated her wish to talk to the great physician; surely he would not abandon her and her child. The matron calmed the distraught girl, assuring her that she would definitely be admitted to the small hospital for the upcoming birth. How could she be so sure, the girl wanted to know. She had begun to cry again; her life seemed to hang so precariously in Dr. Ripley's hands. The woman stood up, tall and confident, and explained to a disbelieving young woman that she was Dr. Ripley and that this was her hospital.

Martha Rogers was born in Vermont on November 30, 1843, to Scotch-Irish parents, the first of five children. Spurred by the lure of cheap western land, the family moved to Iowa to stake its claim while Martha was still an infant. Martha's father was a hard-working farmer who loved politics and served as county supervisor. Her mother was a fierce abolitionist. From them Martha learned her unyielding sense of fairness. Deploring cruelty of any kind, the Rogers family had often aided escaped slaves, even before President Lincoln issued his historic Emancipation Proclamation. Martha was part of this work, too, and she helped by carrying food to runaway slaves.

A beautiful child, Martha was also determined. Though she was taught at home most of her life, she aspired to become a schoolteacher, one of the few professions open to prairie women at the time. She reached her goal while she was still a teenager and began her teaching career in Iowa. As fate would have it, however, her tenure as a school marm was interrupted when a diphtheria epidemic broke out, striking ill many of the settlers in the area. Martha turned from teaching to nursing and began to care for the sick, coaxing them back to good health. She was good at nursing. Wanting to continue in the medical profession, she volunteered as an army nurse when the Civil War broke out. Unfortunately her application was rejected because she was still in her teens and too young to enlist. Not one to take rejection too easily, Martha subsequently volunteered for the U.S. Sanitary Commission and worked hard to solicit gifts and money for Union soldiers. Despite her loveliness and her youth, Martha was a tough taskmaster when it came to recruiting others to help her cause. The story goes that Martha called upon a farmer in the area for a contribution:

"Not a penny," the rich and stingy man replied nastily, "but I will give you all the potatoes you can dig in a day."

"How many hours do you call a day?" she asked.

"From sunup to sundown is the rule on this farm."

"Very well, I will be in your potato field at sunrise."

Martha was a farmer's daughter it was true, but she hadn't engaged in hard physical labor in quite some time. She was however, a very beguiling creature, and she used her persuasive wiles to convince the farmer's wife and daughter to show her where to find the best potatoes and the easiest digging. By 11:00 A.M. she had unearthed so many potatoes that the farmer acquiesced and offered her $10 as his contribution to help the war effort. But Martha kept digging. She still had many more hours to gather potatoes, and they would make good eating for her soldiers. She stopped for just a moment in her work to reply to the shocked farmer.

"If you had given me $5.00 yesterday," she said, "I should have been quite satisfied, but now I am going to have potatoes." When the sun sunk below the horizon that evening, Martha's hands were sore and her back was throbbing, but she had $90 worth of potatoes in her possession.

Martha married William Warren Ripley, a well-to-do Massachusetts man in 1869, and her life took another turn. The young couple moved east so William could manage his uncle's paper mill. Martha gave birth to three children, but she was still determined to pursue humanitarian work outside the home. She joined the growing suffrage movement that had taken hold of the nation's progressive women and also worked tirelessly to help the indigent families of mill workers. One day a baby, very sick with the croup, choked to death while in her care. Martha felt powerless to help the child and at that point decided she would have to study medicine. She found an able mentor in her sister, who had by this time graduated from Boston University School of Medicine.

Martha, now thirty-seven years old, entered the same school in 1880, and from the start she felt as if she had been meant for this type of rigorous study all along. In her second year Martha led a protest rally against an antiquated school policy that forbade women from watching actual operations. Although she was unsuccessful in getting the official rule changed, women were never again barred from operating rooms. She graduated with full honors in 1883, and a faculty member was heard to say that she was "one of the most thorough physicians the school had produced."

But there was tragedy amid her achievement. Martha's husband, William, had an accident at the mill, and because of his injuries, he was forced to stop working. The children were still small and it fell to Martha to support the family. The decision was made to move to Minneapolis, Minnesota, where William had family, and it was here that Dr. Martha Ripley opened her medical practice in obstetrics and children's diseases.

Emboldened by her strong regard for right and wrong and needing to feed a healthy social consciousness, Martha threw herself into reforming her new city. Within six months she was elected president of the Minnesota Woman Suffrage Association. Aligning her group with the temperance movement that was gaining momentum, she was successful in bringing the Seventeenth Annual Convention of the American Woman Suffrage Association to Minneapolis. Other causes she joined were the fight to increase the age of sexual consent for young girls, thus limiting forced marriages; the need for women on the police force; the right for maids to unionize; and the right of women to serve on boards of education. She also was part of the Women's Rescue League and the Minneapolis Improvement League, where she spearheaded a fight against contaminated drinking water.

She still wanted to do more for the poor and unfortunate. Hospital deliveries of babies were uncommon at this time even though extensive professional medical care was often needed for the new mothers and infants. In November 1886, after just three years of practice, Martha established her Maternity Hospital in a small house at 316 Fifteenth Street South. Against the common practice at the time, her facility accepted both married and unmarried mothers and treated those who could afford medical care as well as those who could not.

The demand was so great for services at Martha's hospital that by the end of the first month, its patients had already outgrown the quaint clapboard house. A friend stepped up to help, donating the use of an eighteen-room house, rent free, for six months. The next year, Martha organized a group of women who worked together to buy a residence at 2529 Fourth Avenue South in which to house the growing hospital. Later years would show this acquisition to be just the infancy stage of Ripley's hospital.

The hospital continued to flourish. With its superior facilities and staff, Martha could boast that not one child had been lost during birth. In 1896, just ten years after her hospital had admitted its first expectant mother, a larger house on five acres of land on the corner of Glenwood and Penn Avenues North was purchased.

Here the hospital was to thrive for the next twenty years. Renovations were made as specific demands surfaced: a nursery, a residence for nurses, and a children's ward for isolation cases. The facility was well respected in the area and was among the first hospitals to encourage natural childbirth and cohabitation of mother and newborn. Martha went a step further. She wanted to ensure that her hospital helped women on their road to recovery, so new mothers who found themselves in a sorry state, uneducated or without a job skill to market, were taught sewing, cooking, and other household tasks. Those who had a bent for business were taught stenography. Martha's hospital also acted as an adoption agency for those mothers who wanted to give up their babies after birth in the hopes of providing a better life for these children. Martha also established a social service department, whose mission was to help women with non-medical problems.

The demands of the small hospital continued to grow. On the twenty-fifth anniversary of its founding, Dr. Martha Ripley, always looking for new ways and means to expand her hospital and its services, found herself appealing to the government for an even larger building and $50,000 in funding to come from public sources.

Seeking to raise funds, she spoke out: "Maternity Hospital is more than a hospital. It has been a home and a shelter for deserted wives and widows; for homeless infants and wronged and betrayed girls who needed shelter and skillful care. In all these long years it has been like a wise and loving mother to all who have come through its doors. Many girls have said that it was the only real home they have known. If the good work done by it could be known, there would be no lack of money."

Martha worked long and hard in her hospital, and the care of her patients was of the utmost concern to her and her staff. Under her tutelage the hospital achieved a maternal death rate of 1.35 per thousand, compared to the statewide rate of 4.5 deaths per thousand.

Martha was very successful in the medical field, and she continued to champion the rights of women. She served as president of the Minnesota Woman Suffrage Association, 1883–1888, and worked long and hard for the passage of the Nineteenth Amendment to the Constitution of the United States. She constantly fought against the men and social ills that led to abuse of women and children. She supported laws and ordinances to protect families and end the violence perpetrated against women and children.

Ever vigilant with regard to hospital matters, Martha devoted little time to her own health, choosing to ignore a respiratory infection. She caught a terrible cold while attending an event at the state capitol in the bleak chill of a December evening. She was sick for months and could not seem to shake her illness. By early spring her condition had progressed beyond healing. On April 18, 1912, Martha used her final breath to ask, "Is everything all right at the hospital?"

She left behind a community in grief. Three years later, to commemorate her zeal and passion in the medical field, the name of the hospital she had founded was changed from simply the Maternity Hospital to the Ripley Memorial Foundation Hospital. In 1939 Dr. Martha Ripley was ceremoniously remembered with a plaque in the capitol rotunda of Saint Paul, espousing her commitment to the women of the city. The memorial is etched with these words: "With farsighted vision and sympathy, she served humanity. Fearless in spirit, courageous in action, champion of righteousness, her life was a noble influence, an enduring inspiration."

Medicine has changed much since Martha pioneered her ideas of obstetrics and care for the poor and needy, and one can't help but wonder what has become of the hundreds of babies born under her loving and skillful protection. Where are they now? What have they contributed to this world?

The nameless young woman who was abandoned by her faithless lover became one of Martha's early success stories. Martha explained what happened after she accepted the sobbing, desperate mother-to-be as her patient back in 1886: "The landlord has kindly sent her trunk. She says as soon as she is able she will work and pay back all she owes. This is only one of the many cases, and there are those living and doing well today in our city and state, who but for Maternity's aid would have rushed into eternity."

Ripley Memorial served the Minneapolis area until 1957 when, due to low occupancy and funding problems, the facility shut its doors for the last time. Even with the closure of the hospital, however, Ripley's efforts continue. The hospital structure was sold to Children's Hospital, and the remaining assets were used to create the Ripley Memorial Foundation, a nonprofit charitable organization that promotes the welfare of women and children. Since 1993 the foundation has been a major supporter of teen pregnancy prevention programs. This continued commitment would have made Martha proud of her profession and of the city that for so many years supported her humanitarian efforts.

FRANCES DENSMORE

1867–1957

American Ethnomusicologist

*O*pening day attendees trembled with excitement as they entered the gates of the Chicago World's Columbian Exposition that warm, sunny day in May 1893, winding their way past the immense Administration Building and gliding into the open Court of Honor. Invitations to attend this event had been spread out across the United States and into the far corners of the globe. It was to be a huge event, greater even than the Paris Exposition Universale of 1889.

Newspapers across the country chronicled the events leading up to the exhibition's opening for months. Chicago businessmen Andrew McNally, George Pullman, and J. P. Morgan had put up enormous sums of money so the Windy City could serve as host to the "once in a lifetime" spectacular. There had been much talk about how the fair would be set in Jackson Park, a peaceful area on the banks of Lake Michigan. Many couldn't wait to see how architect Frederick Law Olmstead, designer of New York's Central Park, would create man-made lagoons, waterways, and reflecting pools to soothe the frazzled fairgoers.

As opening day drew near, reports were replete with the news

LIBRARY OF CONGRESS, LC-USZ62-107289

Frances Densmore and Mountain Chief

that President Cleveland would be present to pull the gilded lever to start the festivities. No one could have guessed, however, that before the exposition ended six months later, it would have accommodated more than twenty-seven million visitors from all over the world.

The days were blisteringly hot as visitors filed into Machinery Hall and the Palace of Fine Arts, found their way to Wooded Island, and enjoyed many of the Midway's attractions. But the most popular exhibit was the Electricity Building, a six-acre expanse of incredible modernity. It was easy to see why. The huge building was bathed in bright electrical light, more brilliant than any spectator at the time could have conceived. Moses P. Handy's publicity guidebook was justified in its boast that Thomas Edison's eighty-two-foot Tower of Light was made up of more than 18,000 light bulbs. Inside the hall were the technological marvels of a new era: sewing machines, burglar alarms, seismographs, and more of the latest innovations from electrical lights to weather stations.

The fair fervor eventually reached the small, frontier town of Red Wing, Minnesota, and twenty-six-year-old Frances Densmore seized the opportunity to attend the Native American presentations that drew her interest. She was naively unaware of how the technology exhibit would play a significant role in her future. Looking back years later, Frances would mark the World's Columbian Exposition of 1893 as the beginning of her lifelong career. Surely she felt that something was in the air, something new and different, something that would make a difference to her life.

Frances Theresa was born on May 21, 1867, in Red Wing, a small southeastern Minnesota town set amid giant limestone bluffs with names like Sorin Bluff and Barn Bluff, where Henry David Thoreau had climbed in 1861 to write about the splendor of the landscape. The town lay in a sharp but quiet bend of the Mississippi River and was home to migratory birds and wild ducks, beautiful seasonal flowers, and vast prairies. Red Wing was supported by the rich farmland surrounding it, and Goodhue County topped the state's list of grain-producing areas. By the time Frances was born, Red Wing was a fast-growing port for grain shipments and home to many wealthy mill owners, lumber barons, and business-savvy merchants.

Frances's prominent grandparents had settled in the area after a westward trek across country from New York. Grandfather Orrin Densmore was superintendent of a local sawmill and participated in many educational efforts in the small town. He was quite a colorful character who dabbled in science and held a job preparing monthly local weather reports for the Smithsonian Institute in Washington, D.C. Frances's father, Benjamin, was a civil engineer who served in the Sixth Minnesota Regiment during the Civil War. After the war he and his brother Daniel founded the Red Wing Iron Works. In 1866 Benjamin married Sarah Adelaide Greenland, and the next year Frances was born.

In the late 1800s Red Wing was still a frontier settlement. Tepees dotted the land just beyond the town limits. As she was growing up, Frances was accustomed to seeing Indians walking the streets of her town. She developed a keen curiosity and always wanted to know more about these "strange people." Early on, she was intrigued by the music she heard filtering out from the Indian village near her home. She wrote later: "Our home commanded a view of the Mississippi River. Opposite the town, on an island, was a camp of Sioux Indians and at night, when they were dancing, we could hear the sound of the drum and see the flicker of camp-fire. In the twilight I listened to these sounds, when I ought to have been going to sleep."

Music was to be a part of her life from the start. Frances began her musical education at a young age, and as her training was classical in nature, she was sternly reprimanded if she attempted to play anything considered frivolous. She endured this strenuous musical education, and at just seventeen years of age was sent far from her Minnesota home to Oberlin Conservatory in Ohio, where she studied piano, organ, and harmony. After graduation in 1887 she traveled east to Boston, where she studied with composer Carl Baermann and renowned composer and Harvard professor John Knowles Paine. A bright addendum to her musical studies at this time came in the form of her fortunate discovery of Alice Cunningham Fletcher and Fletcher's work recording the music of the Omaha Indians.

After two winters in Boston, Frances returned home to set up a studio and teach piano. It was about this time that she began seeing articles in the local newspaper touting the upcoming Chicago fair. She made the fortuitous decision to attend, eagerly packed her suitcase, and headed to the World's Columbian Exposition of 1893. It was here that the new, lightweight version of Edison's 1877 sound recording machine caught her attention. Frances had already entertained the idea of studying Indian music during her days in Boston reading Fletcher's research. She was now spurred on once again and lost no time obtaining a copy of Fletcher's *A Study of Omaha Music*, which had recently been published. This text would serve as the inspiration for her own work, but whereas Fletcher had roamed the countryside recording Omaha music with a crude, unmanageable device, Frances saw the potential in Edison's compact recording invention.

Stirred by all the exciting things she had seen at the world's fair, Frances headed back to Red Wing and began to formalize her plan to study and record Indian music. The academic world was just beginning to recognize the importance of preserving the music of Indian cultures—many tribes, and their cultures, were fast disappearing because of the white man's determination to "civilize" them. She wanted to record their tribal music before it was no more. She packed again for another trip, this time to the Milwaukee School of Music to visit John Comfort Fillmore, a collaborator of Fletcher's and transcriber of her recorded Native American songs. His piano accompaniments and complex harmonizations were to have considerable influence on Frances's own studies.

Frances immediately began to study Indian lore and history in-depth, while still giving piano lessons and acting as her church choral leader. She immersed herself in her studies, reading Fletcher's book over and over again, as well as anything else she could get her hands on about Indian life, music, or customs. She was excited to be corresponding with Fletcher and was already making a name for herself lecturing to local town groups on both classical music and Fletcher's research. She took her work of disseminating information on Indian culture very seriously. She attended elocution lessons to improve her diction and included musical accompaniment in her lectures, striking two sticks together to give the illusion of a drum sound. It was not long before she was traveling to North Dakota, Illinois, and New York to deliver her lectures. By 1903 she had a real drum, an authentic Indian tom-tom with its soft deerskin cover, and four birch-bark rattles used by the Chippewa medicine men in their rituals. She used these instruments to enrich her recitals and lectures. Frances also embarked on a writing career and published an article, "The Song and the Silence of the Red Man," in the *Minneapolis Journal*.

In 1905 Frances was ready for another bold adventure, but this time she would not go alone. Her sister Margaret would serve as her traveling companion. The Densmores boarded a small passenger boat from a Duluth pier on the shore of Lake Superior. As it set sail north, both women were excited to be making their first trip to a Chippewa Indian village at Grand Marais. On their arrival Frances was able to make arrangements with an Indian guide named Caribou to show them around the town. But that was not what

Frances really wanted to see. She was ultimately able to convince Caribou to take the sisters out to meet the Chippewa medicine man, Shingibis, who lived beyond the town, deep in the Minnesota woods. Shingibis agreed to hold a religious ceremony and allowed Frances and her sister to listen to the ceremonial songs. The Indians sang well into the night, and Frances was so awed by the experience that she dared not take out her notebook to record the music she was hearing. Leaving Shingibis and Grand Marais, Frances and Margaret next visited Grand Portage, home to another band of Chippewa. Here, as she moved among the welcoming Indians, Frances felt comfortable enough to make some small lantern slides that would serve as invaluable visuals for future lectures.

Frances was busy trying to record all the songs she was hearing at the various Indian villages she and Margaret visited, but her transcriptions lacked the authenticity of the Indian voice. As she again packed for a trip, this time to the White Earth Reservation in western Minnesota, Frances held on to a secret hope that someday one of the Indians would trust her enough to sing into a recording machine.

White Earth was a sprawling community made up of small farms, numerous homes with adjacent vegetable gardens, and a small schoolhouse. The Ojibwe who lived here were known for the delicious jams and jellies that they preserved so well. One little girl had boasted how her father was a great deer hunter, and when he returned from his hunt, he would tell her where she could find the best wild fruit that he had seen on his travels. Another treat the reservation produced was the wonderful sugar cakes made from sap collected from the local maple trees. Frances loved the smell coming from the vats of sugary substance boiling down from a thin, watery liquid to thick golden brown syrup. Although the White Earth Reservation had many elders, both men and women, unlike some ethnomusicologists, Frances made sure to include many lullabies and children's songs in her research. Frances tried to befriend as many community members as she could. Though the women kept to their cooking, laundry, and basket making and the men were wary of her intentions, Frances managed to make a great many friends. Imagine her great surprise when one of the Indians agreed to record tribal songs by singing into a recording device. Their relationship flourished, and Frances was able to persuade Big Bear, as he was called, to sing his heart out. She made arrangements to borrow the needed recording equipment from a local music store and persuaded the owner to let her set up a studio in his back room. Big Bear's songs filled twelve cylinder records, some of which are now on depository with the Library of Congress in Washington, D.C.

Frances believed strongly in her mission, and while feeling privileged to have witnessed a traditional funeral ritual and feast while visiting a reservation at Leech Lake, she realized she had a lot of work yet to do. She appealed to the Bureau of American Ethnology at the Smithsonian Institution for funds to help pay some of her expenses. With the $150 she received, Frances bought one of the Edison machines, a Columbia Graphophone, a recording device she had first heard calling out to her in the Hall of Electricity nearly ten years earlier.

Frances was now geared for action. She had studied relentlessly and lectured and recorded and transcribed and made friends with many of the Indians. Now, with her new recording machine, she was ready to embark on professional fieldwork, gathering musical recordings, firsthand, from Native Americans across the state. The Bureau of American Ethnology described her work in its 1907–1908 annual report: "The collection of phonographic records so far obtained is extensive, and the investigation promises results of exceptional interest and scientific value."

During the next year Frances became very popular on the lecture circuit. When she addressed the Anthropological Society of Washington in 1908, she was thrilled to learn that her mentor and inspiration, Alice Fletcher, was in the audience. Frances had written to Fletcher for years, seeking advice and help with her work, but words could not express how excited she was to finally meet her professional friend face-to-face. Her passion for preserving the music of the Indians was fueled by this meeting, and she rededicated herself to her work. Though she was happy that some of the Indians had stepped forward to share their music with the white man, she sympathized with their increasing loss of heritage and history. She put these feelings into words in one of her 1912 lectures: "We have taken from the Indian his land and his hunting ground, but he is carrying his song with him, on his last long journey. Strange as it may seem the Indian is willing to give his songs."

Frances lived a long life recording the music of the Indian tribes she loved so well, and she was not content to stay within the Minnesota territory she called home. Her travels and studies took her far beyond those boundaries. Besides the Chippewa she also studied the Teton Sioux, Northern Ute, the Tule Indians of Panama, Papago, Pawnee, the Yuman and Yaqui, Seminole, Cheyenne and Arapaho, and some Pueblo tribes—always recording, always learning, always searching for the soul of the people within their music.

Frances grew old following her heart and never stopped dreaming of ways to preserve the tribal customs and music she felt were such a part of American lore. In 1948, because of a generous grant, the Federal government began the task of protecting Frances's work by transferring her wax cylinder recordings to permanent disks. Though she was eighty-one at the time, Frances agreed to supervise the project from her home in Red Wing, Minnesota. As if this were not enough, she also busied herself selecting some of her most favorite Indian pieces to be put on long-playing records that for the first time would be made available to the public.

When these projects were completed, Frances, even at eighty-seven years old, was still not done. In 1954 she lectured in a seminar series at the University of Florida in Gainesville. While in the Sunshine State, she worked among the Seminoles in the area to unearth important, and as yet, unrecorded data.

Frances died on June 5, 1957, in Red Wing; she was ninety years old. The sleepy town, tucked away in its sheltering bend of the Mississippi River, had not changed all that much in her lifetime. One could still meander down to the St. James Hotel with its beautiful limestone walls or visit Christ Episcopal Church that had added a new Parish Hall back in 1911. The post office was still housed in its 1910 building, and the Red Wing Shoe Company continued making quality shoes. But, oh, had the world changed around it. The World's Columbian Exposition of 1893 was now just a footnote in history, but the technological revolution it showcased ushered in a new and remarkable age. Frances had glimpsed the future of the world in the glittering lights of Edison's tower, and her own life would be marked by the discoveries that were yet to come.

Thanks to the efforts of Frances Densmore, Native American music and culture is preserved for future generations to study and enjoy. Frances recorded more than 2,500 songs, plus many other musical pieces, from more than thirty tribes onto wax cylinders. Her entire collection was eventually transferred to long-playing records for the Smithsonian-Densmore Collection of Indian Sound Recordings. She had also collected hundreds of musical instruments that are now housed in the Smithsonian. By the time of her death, Frances had published more than twenty books and 200 articles on Indian music, culture, customs, and life. She can rightfully be called an American pioneer in ethnomusicology.

LIANG MAY SEEN
1871–1946

Activist and
Friend to Immigrants

*L*iang May Seen stared at the small urban house before her. It was so unlike the sprawling home she had known as a young girl growing up in southern China's Pearl River Delta! She knew she should stop the flood of unreachable childhood dreams, right now, right here. She must enter her new home with a clear mind and a sincere spirit. But the summer day was warm, especially for Minnesota, and May Seen couldn't keep herself from thinking back to earlier times spent among family and friends in her beloved China, now just a distant memory. Though she was only twenty-one years old, her days of wide-eyed innocence had been buried years ago under the weight of her constant fight for survival in this strange country called America. A light breeze blew against her cheek, steamy and humid, reviving familiar images of her village, Kaiping, nicknamed "Little Wuhan" to celebrate its wonderfully colorful gardens. She remembered the hot afternoons she had spent lazily watching water buffalo as they plowed through the muddy fields of her homeland. Her thoughts drifted to the

WOO FAMILY, MINNESOTA HISTORICAL SOCIETY

Liang May Seen and her husband Woo Yee Sing

famous Paradise of Birds refuge and the legend of how the sanc-
tuary began more than 500 years ago when a simple farmer put a
banyan tree branch into the Tanma River to fasten his boat. Over
the years the branch had grown into a tree, and with the passing of
time, the conditions of the once-poor villagers had improved
tremendously. People came to believe the tree was holy, and when-
ever they passed it, they threw handfuls of dirt around its base. The
small land area in the river expanded and flourished; it first became
an islet and then widened into a lush woodland. More than 40,000
white crannies and gray-pocked cranes call the Paradise of Birds their
home. May Seen shook the image of these beautiful flocking birds
out of her head. Her carefree days of playing around the farmhouses
on the road to Xinhui were just elusive images now, as was the com-
forting statue of the Buddha that had sat in a temple high on a hill-
top behind her home, a beloved spirit of a far-away past.

May Seen glanced down again at the small photograph she
had carried all the way from San Francisco. It showed a Chinese
couple in long, brocade Chinese robes staring straight ahead at the
camera, expressionless. The petite woman is standing with her hand
resting on the arm of the chair in which the man next to her is
seated. The photographer had asked the man to sit down because
he was so much taller than the woman. The two people are neither
touching nor smiling; they are showing little emotion. Yet they are
wearing traditional marriage gowns. Looking at the photo, May
Seen smiled a knowing smile. The lanky man was her husband now
and she was his new wife. May Seen was about to embark on a
great adventure and that meant starting a new life with this strange
man she hardly knew. She would never forget her past; that is the
curse and blessing of being an immigrant. Memories of her
beloved home would color most everything she would do in this
new world. Entering the small but welcoming house as a married
woman for the first time would put into motion a series of events

that May Seen could never have imagined. She was ready to begin. She would pass into the annals of history as the first woman of Chinese descent to live in Minnesota . . . ever!

Liang May Seen was born in 1871 in the Kaiping District of southern China's Guandong Province. Though the area was known for its fragrant and verdant gardens and the nearby seaport was bustling, the farmers toiled under a strict government regime that allowed them little more than a meager subsistence.

May Seen's story was not unlike that of other young girls of the area. Her family was very poor, with no hope of eking out a better future. Her destitute father had no choice: In 1885, when May Seen was just fourteen years old, her father sold her to a San Francisco–based marriage broker. This procurer had assured May Seen's mother that when her daughter arrived in America she would be wed to a man from the Kaiping District who had emigrated years earlier looking for fame and fortune in the West. He was a man of substance and wealth, the broker said, and would take good care of May Seen.

The husband-to-be was one of many adventurous single men who had departed from the area in droves for years; 25,000 Chinese men had arrived in California with Gold Rush fever in 1851 alone. The men had come to the new land as pioneers of their own free will, not enslaved or shackled. They hoped to make enough money to proudly return home and care for their families. They built railroads, aqueducts, bridges, levees, and wineries. They were part of the work force that was moving and shaping the young country. Though Chinese immigration had fallen off since the economic depression of the 1880s and with the passage of the 1882 Exclusion Act, a considerable number of eligible Chinese men were looking for wives from their hometowns.

May Seen's family was satisfied to receive the small pittance in return for sending their daughter across the ocean. They awaited the announcement of her marriage to a rich merchant, who would be willing and able to send money back to China to support the family. It had been done many times before, and ample evidence of the wealth sent back from America was visible in some of the nice homes sprouting up in the countryside and towns of the area. So, to do her part to help out, young May Seen wiped her tears away and waved a final good-bye to the family she loved so much. In her youthful exuberance it didn't enter her mind that she might never see them again.

After about a month at sea on the crowded ship, May Seen began searching the approaching California coastline for *Gum San*, the "gold mountain" some of the passengers had told her about. It was a land of great fortune they had explained. She was trying to find something to smile about, and a golden mountain would surely raise her spirits. Again, she wiped away her tears, hoping this would be the last time she would be so weak. She allowed herself to think back to her beloved China so far away now and a chill crept across her neck. She felt very scared and very alone.

May Seen had a right to be frightened. There was no gold mountain in California, and the glory days of plentiful work and social acceptance were over for the Chinese immigrants. The men who had worked so hard and so long to make their way in the New World were blamed for taking jobs away from Americans. Now they were forced to do menial work to survive and were generally looked upon with disdain. Many decided to change the course of their lives and fled from the newly formed anti-Asian mobs and their daily attacks. They dispersed inland and eastward to the American Midwest. Here, separated from the close-knit communities they had known in California, they faced limited opportunities, language barriers, and racial discrimination. The wholesome environment May Seen had been promised no longer existed. And what was worse, the broker entrusted with the life of young May Seen was not legitimate. Instead of meeting the rich man the procurer had promised, May Seen was sold to a brothel in San Francisco's Chinatown. It would take her four long years to escape her horrific ordeal.

Knowing there was no one who could help her out of this unfortunate situation but herself, May Seen had kept her eyes and ears open, willing herself to survive and preparing for the day she could escape her servitude. She had heard about a Presbyterian Mission Home in the city, founded in 1874, and supported by the Women's Occidental Board of Foreign Missions that took in young women who were alone and destitute. When her plans to get out of the brothel were complete, she sent a message to the mission detailing her escape, hoping her plea for help would fall on understanding ears. She intended to slip away after singing at a merchant's banquet in a well-known Chinatown restaurant that evening. Knowing that she would be spotted and captured if she did not get away quickly, May Seen described an intersection near the restaurant that she knew she could reach. She hoped someone would be there to meet her. Margaret Culbertson, superintendent of the home, also knew her actions had to be swift and expedient. She had rescued many young women like May Seen before. Without hesitation she ordered a horse and carriage and sped to the designated meeting place. May Seen found her way to the shadowy intersection, boarded the carriage that had been waiting for her, and fled the dismal streets of Chinatown forever.

"The Home," as it was called by the locals, was heaven to May Seen. She gratefully immersed herself in the daily requirements: class work, household chores, and religious activities. The mission was supported by many Presbyterians churches throughout the country, and May Seen was just one of 400 young women rescued from the streets of San Francisco in its first twenty years of operation. During her three-year respite at "The Home," May Seen learned English, sewing, and math, and converted to Christianity. But everything was not perfect; something was lacking in her life. May Seen was twenty-one years old and unmarried. Then Woo Yee Sing came into her life.

Yee Sing was from the same Kaiping District as May Seen. He had been eighteen years old when he came seeking his fortune in California, believing the tall tales of fame and opportunity he had heard. But by the time he arrived, San Francisco was rife with anti-Chinese violence and so, dismayed and dejected, he had traveled across the country looking for a more hospitable area. In 1882 Yee Sing became the first Chinese man to settle permanently in Minneapolis, joining only twenty-four other Chinese in the state who were living in Duluth, Saint Paul, and the Iron Range region. By 1890 the number of Chinese immigrants had inched up to ninty-four, all men, most seeking to change their status from laborer to small businessman. In an effort to escape the Exclusion Act that threatened to deport laborers who did not own property, the men had taken up professions such as hotel managers, restaurant owners, import shopkeepers, grocery store clerks, and businesses that no one else wanted—especially laundries. Chinese laundries were typically small, unventilated spaces where temperatures would climb near one hundred degrees, and where the workers often developed health problems such as ulcers, internal bleeding, tuberculosis, and swollen feet. The boiling process in the cramped and steamy environment was nearly intolerable, and all ironing was done by hand with steel irons that weighed eight pounds, causing blisters and, eventually, thick calluses to ravage the hands.

Yee Sing was a hard worker and a determined man, and though it seemed a harsh future, he jumped at the chance to open a small hand laundry in Minneapolis. Fortuitously for May Seen, it was near the city's Westminster Presbyterian Church.

Yee Sing was no stranger to Westminster. In 1883 he went to the church to see if he could find someone who would teach him English. A Mrs. Harris volunteered, and so began the opening chapter of the Westminster Chinese Sunday School. It wasn't long before Yee Sing converted to Christianity and became a part of the Westminster Church community. Yee Sing was a good business-man. He was able to bring over his younger brother, and in 1883 they opened Canton Restaurant, the first Chinese eatery in Min-neapolis. It was now time for him to find a wife. He had heard of the Presbyterian Mission Home in San Francisco and planned his trip to find a bride. He kept his appointment with Margaret Cul-bertson, who found his credentials to be firm and his Christianity true. Mrs. Culbertson approved of the serious young man, and so did Liang May Seen. The couple was married at "The Home" on July 21, 1892.

And here she was at the threshold of a new home and a new direction in life. May Seen put the wedding photograph away and walked proudly through the front door of the small Grant Street house Yee Sing had bought. She was the first and only Chinese woman in Minneapolis, she knew with that unique title came a responsibility to help those who were surely to follow in her foot-steps, those others who would also be seeking asylum and warmth from the thriving Midwestern town she would forever more call home. It would be years before restrictions on bringing Chinese wives into the United States were lifted, but she would commit herself to showing all newcomers the same kindness she had expe-rienced in the mission home in San Francisco and the warm friend-ship that had seen her through the hard times of settling into a new and different society.

While Yee Sing and his brother prospered in their businesses, May Seen was preparing for her own business debut. She was a very busy woman. She played an active role in the Westminster Presbyterian Church, attending its English-speaking services every Sunday; she took English lessons to improve the language she had started to learn at the home; and she pursued an education in math to help her with her new business idea. In 1904 she opened a Chinese curio shop next to the new church. In 1896 the Westminister Church had moved down Nicollet Avenue to a beautiful brick edifice with enough room to house all its church-related programs. May Seen could not help but be impressed with its massive size and regal architectural elements. Her store was an immediate hit, and her reputation as an avid and trusted church member guaranteed its success. During her first ten years in Minneapolis, May Seen made a great many allies among native Minnesotans. She counted as her friends Lenore Cunnington, head of the Chinese school; Ella and Annette Holsted, missionaries to China; and many others. But after ten years of being the sole Chinese woman in the city, she was elated to learn that someone from her home district of Kaiping would finally be arriving. Minnie Wong, bride of laundry operator Wong Gee, became a lifelong friend and fellow volunteer in May Seen's work with Chinese immigrants.

One sad note during this time was that May Seen and Yee Sing were unable to have children. Though May Seen often helped other women with their children, she longed for a child of her own. The love that May Seen and Yee Sing had for each other had grown and flourished from the very first day they had met, and it would see them through this disappointment. In 1906 the couple traveled to San Francisco to adopt a baby boy. The process was facilitated with the help of Donaldina Cameron, recently promoted from assistant to superintendent of "The Home." May Seen had known Donaldina when she was assistant to Margaret Culbertson. Over the last few years, the women had corresponded and become good friends. The boy was named Howard, and he would one day become an architect of note in Minneapolis.

The Westminster Chinese Sunday School eventually opened its doors to women in 1920 after having provided Chinese men with an education in English for nearly forty years. May Seen and her friend Minnie Wong were on the top of the list of volunteers to help tutor the new students. Their roles expanded and they were called on to help the new émigrés with any problems they might have trying to adjust to their new lives. With May Seen's help the new immigrants established organizations within the church structure that focused on forming supportive relationships for the newcomers. May Seen could not forget how she had been helped when she had first arrived in this country and how she had been welcomed by the women of Westminster. She became a mentor to young women, encouraging them to participate in church functions as well as join some of the outside groups in the larger society.

May Seen and Yee Sing wanted to tell everyone how much they appreciated the city's warmth and friendliness, and so they started a long tradition of hosting a lavish Chinese banquet to honor the community in which they lived and worked. The guest list included the governor, the mayor, and other local dignitaries, as well as pastors from various churches, businesspeople, and friends. The overwhelming annual attendance was a testament to the couple's appreciation of the kindness shown them by friends and business acquaintances. The years in Minneapolis had been fruitful and the couple could boast of owning three hand laundries, two restaurants, an import business, and a curio shop in the heart of the city.

In 1925 after thirty years of marriage, May Seen lost her devoted husband and life partner, Yee Sing. On the way to the cemetery, May Seen turned around to look at the long line of cars behind her in the funeral procession. So many people, she thought, and not for the first time in her marriage, she realized how fortunate she had been to have married Yee Sing. The long, lonely voyage across the ocean, the terrible days in San Francisco, and the arduous trip to Minneapolis had been worth the effort. Newspapers the following day published glowing reports about the perfect blending of Chinese and American customs during the solemn funeral ceremony and described the countless bouquets that adorned the beloved man's coffin as it passed through the streets of Minneapolis going from the church to the cemetery.

After her husband's death, and her son's marriage, May Seen threw herself further into community work. She was persistent in her commitment to intercultural friendship. She worked for another twenty years and saw many changes. She lived to see a repeal of the immigration laws that had excluded the Chinese.

Liang May Seen died in 1946 at the age of seventy-five. She had blazed a trail and left her legacy to two young friends who served as active advocates for women in the Chinese-American community. When the restrictions in the War Brides Act of 1945 were lifted, approximately 8,000 Chinese wives of servicemen were allowed to enter the United States. Many came to the Minneapolis area and attended the English-language classes at the Westminster Presbyterian Church, not held just on Sundays now but during the week as well. A strong advocate for women from the turn of the century until the 1940s, Liang May Seen has been called a model for young Chinese women. She encouraged Chinese-American women to become active in their communities, especially in their churches, and she spent countless hours helping the new arrivals. She was a wife, mother, business partner, business owner, active church member, and an activist who worked long and hard to further social acceptance of Chinese Americans. Liang May Seen had journeyed far and accomplished much. Her story is part of America's history of immigration and assimilation and is housed in the Minnesota, Historical Collection in Minneapolis. Dr. Sarah Refo

Mason in her study of the Chinese immigrants in Minnesota has called Liang May Seen "instrumental in developing a prosperous and nurturing environment for Chinese Americans" in Minnesota's "richly diverse history of growth and change."

FANNY
FLIGELMAN BRIN
1884–1961

Suffragette and Campaigner
for World Peace

*P*resident of the United States Harry S. Truman walked up to the podium and quietly waited for the buzz running through the large conference room to subside. He began his address to the imposing audience in a strong and confident voice:

> Delegates to the United Nations Conference on International Organization. . .

Fanny sat very still; she found it hard to believe she was actually in the presence of such a great man. The excitement in the room was growing, but the seriousness of the occasion quieted the crowd, and Truman's words reached the far corners of the room. He continued:

> At no time in history has there been a more important Conference, nor a more necessary meeting, than this one in San Francisco. . . .

GENE GARRETT, MINNESOTA HISTORICAL SOCIETY

Fanny Fligelman Brin

Fanny thought for a moment of her home in Minnesota, and her long trip west to the "Golden State." People had been saying this was the perfect site for such a momentous meeting because California had always symbolized new beginnings and bright futures. The president's words broke into her reverie:

> On behalf of the American people, I extend to you a hearty welcome.

Fanny, proud of her American allegiance, though she had not been born here, looked around the room and noted the representatives of various nations in attendance: France, the United Kingdom, Australia, the Soviet Union, Canada, Ethiopia. There were representatives from fifty-one of the world's countries, large and small, powerful and fragile, and their distinguished delegates were straining to catch the president's every word:

> You members of this Conference are to be the architects of the better world. In your hands rests our future. By your labors at this Conference, we shall know if suffering humanity is to achieve a just and lasting peace.

And so began, on April 25, 1945, the history-making conference that would set into motion the organization of worldwide cooperation known as the United Nations. Fanny was honored to be a part of this great convocation. She had been chosen as an official alternate for the Women's Action Committee for Lasting Peace, one of only five women's groups invited to the conference by the State Department. She had worked relentlessly back home in Minnesota for world peace, and she could not have been prouder to represent her organization's lofty ideals. She was also serving as observer for the National Council of Jewish Women (NCJW), a group that also looked hopefully forward to the birth of the United Nations. Her generation had lived through two world wars, and citizens and governments alike were still reeling in the aftermath. Surely, Fanny thought, world peace is possible, and within her soul was the faith that everyone in attendance in that room on that important day felt the same optimism. She listened as Secretary of State Edward R. Stettinius Jr. officially opened the conference.

> Now the deepest hope and highest purpose of all mankind—enduring peace—is here committed to our hands. . . . With the conviction that the work we have to do is good and that our purpose can be brought to pass, let us unite with confidence and hope in our common labor.

Fanny Xeriffa was one of seven children born to John Fligelman and his wife Antoinette Friedman. Born on October 20, 1884, in Berlad, Romania, she was only three months old when her parents decided to protect their large family and leave behind the persecutions and bigotry of their mother country. Many had already fled; some had crossed the great ocean seeking a new life in America. John's brother Herman had left two years earlier, settling down in the growing frontier town of Minneapolis. The first Eastern Europeans had arrived unexpectedly in 1882 at the Saint Paul train depot. The refugees were immediately helped by concerned citizens and housed temporarily in tents. By the end of the year, nearly 600 Jewish immigrants had arrived in the city. Although they clung to their Old-World customs and spoke Yiddish for the most part, the immigrants began the difficult and lengthy process of trying to adjust to a new home. German Jews who had settled in the eastern part of the United States had moved westward, seeking new opportunities in which to invest their hard-earned savings. Most had become traders or shopkeepers. They were living in Minnesota when it was created as a territory in 1849, and by 1856, two years before Minnesota became a state, they had formed the Mount Zion Hebrew Association. A synagogue was built a few years later. Although these settled Jews were different and already acculturated to frontier life, they did offer a familiar solace and fellowship to the newcomers. And so when John arrived with his family in 1884 he joined a well-established Jewish community.

John was different from most of the other immigrants. He realized right away that he and his family would have to change quickly in order to survive in this new country. He demanded that all his children speak "American." Even at the dinner table, Yiddish was not acceptable. While John was immersing himself in his new city, he also insisted on teaching fundamental Jewish values and the pursuit of knowledge to his children. Fanny learned the Torah and *tzedakah*, a strong Jewish belief in the importance of helping the less fortunate.

Fanny was a serious child, a resolute student, and early on she demonstrated a political bent inherited from her father. She attended South High School in Minneapolis, a relatively new public school built on a former haymarket site in 1893 due to an increasing student population in the area. Here she began to develop the effective communications skills for which she would be famous later in her career. One of her favorite school activities was participating on the debate team. American Jews were known for their concern with intellectual pursuits and education; they emphasized learning, intellectuality, articulateness, and argument, even argumentativeness. Fanny so loved the craft of argumentative speech that she also joined the debate team while studying at the University of Minnesota. She was the first woman to succeed in the famed Pillsbury oratorical contest, winning a second prize of

$50 for the topic "Russian Bureaucracy and the Jews." Active in the Minerva Literature Society and a member of the Phi Beta Kappa Honor Society, she graduated in 1906 with a B.A. degree.

Fanny went straight to work teaching school. Her first position was at Northfield, and then she moved to West High School in Minneapolis. The world for a Jewish woman in the early years of the twentieth century was full of contradictions. Many women were still trying to learn how to adjust their Old-World traditions to new-world geography and modern ways of thinking. Women had to learn new roles and figure out how to establish Jewish homes despite the obstacles of frontier living.

In isolated areas homesteaders had to rely on shipments of kosher meat in uncooled railroad cars. The meat often arrived unfit to eat. Some families could only maintain kosher for the eight days of Passover using the ritual as a symbol of the year-round devotion that they could not follow. Jewish women had to learn to cook American food to feed their families. Many Jewish women assuaged their frustrations at not being able to follow traditional rituals within the home by increasing their emphasis on other cherished Jewish values. They took seriously their commitment to social responsibility and became involved in religious education, philanthropy, and other organizational work.

Though pressures for rapid Americanization were great and anti-Semitic sentiments were in place, many families were doing very well. Statistics for 1910 show that 87 percent of Jewish girls remained in school until the age of fifteen, a tribute to the prosperity of Jewish families in Minneapolis, despite legal and extra-legal exclusion. Jews were barred from organizations like the Kiwanis, Lions, Minneapolis Athletic Club, Rotary, and social country clubs, which reserved the right to limit membership to a "selected clientele." Limits were imposed on where they could work and go to school, and even on where they could live. It disturbed

Fanny to see narrow-mindedness all around her. And knowing that her family had left Romania to escape some of these same prejudices made her eager to fight for change.

Fanny traced her interest in women's rights to her university days. One of her early inspirations was Frances Squire Potter, an English professor at the University of Minnesota who served as corresponding secretary of the National American Woman Suffrage Association. She also cited as her role models the strong-willed Maud Stockwell, president of the Minnesota Woman Suffrage Association and chairwoman of the Minnesota section of the Women's International League for Peace and Freedom; and Clara Ueland, founder of the Woman's Club of Minneapolis and first president of the Minnesota League of Women Voters in 1919.

Amid her involvement in voluntary activism, Fanny found time to indulge in romance. She met Chicago-born Arthur Brin, who had lived in Minneapolis since infancy. He had started his career as an office boy and was now a successful businessman who owned the Brin Glass Company. Fanny married Arthur Brin on March 19, 1913. Arthur and Fanny were kindred spirits. He was as involved as she was in community affairs, though perhaps he was slightly more conservative than she was. Their first child, a daughter named Rachel, was born in 1915. Son Howard followed in 1919, and a second son, Charles, in 1923.

During the 1920s and 1930s, Fanny was especially active in the National Council of Jewish Women (NCJW), which had been founded in Chicago in 1893 by Hannah G. Solomon to address the concerns of American Jewish women. It provided spiritual, educational, and philanthropic activities and campaigned for women's rights, including the right to vote. Nina Morais Cohen, who had been present at the national organization's creation, established the Minneapolis section just a year later. Nina extended a hand of friendship to young people. She held rigorous NCJW study sessions in her home and invited immigrant women who exhibited leadership abilities to join her, teaching them how to write reports and deliver speeches. Fanny was proud to have been one of Nina's disciples and was excited to serve as director of the Minneapolis Women's Committee for World Disarmament for NCJW. In 1924 she was elected president of the Minneapolis section of the NCJW.

Fanny and Arthur and their growing family lived in a middle-class neighborhood at the south end of town. As active members of the Adath Jeshurun synagogue, they were led by its first American-trained rabbi, C. David Matt. Matt had studied at the Jewish Theological Seminary of America, the center founded by the father of Nina Cohen, Fanny's friend and mentor from the NCJW. All services were conducted in English, and the Orthodox congregation, founded in 1884, was making a bold move toward Conservatism. The Brins were in the thick of organizing this powerful third force in American Jewry that was struggling to fill the gap between old and new, Orthodox and Reform, attitudes. Thanks to the work of many families, including the Brins, Adath Jeshrun became an important focal point in the community; it was clearly central to the Brins' life in Minneapolis.

There were many organizations available in Minneapolis to give Jewish women an opportunity to demonstrate leadership, showcase their business talents, and wield power. Fanny participated in a number of them. The League of Women Voters welcomed Jewish women, and Fanny signed up. In 1930 she became the first woman member appointed to the Minnesota State Teachers College Board. One of the highlights of her career came in 1932 when she was named by Eleanor Roosevelt to a national women's committee to aid social service work.

Fanny felt privileged to work with nationally revered women such as Jane Addams and Carrie Chapman Catt. Catt had already

made a name for herself as key coordinator of the woman's suffrage movement and founder of the League of Women Voters.
Now that women had been given the right to vote, Catt had turned
her energies toward world peace, founding the National Committee on the Cause and Cure of War. Fanny was closely associated
with Catt during the organization's founding and became active in
its activities to achieve world peace. Fanny further worked toward
this end, serving as chairman of the NCJW's International Relations and Peace Committee. Her pacifist ideas were published in an
article for the *Saturday Post*, a Jewish newspaper: "We must not seek
to modify war, but to outlaw it; to make it an international crime."
Her peer and co-worker in the fight for peace Carrie Catt named
Fanny as one of ten outstanding women in 1934. Fanny was active
in other antiwar groups and opposed compulsory military training.
Under her chairmanship of the Committee on Peace and Arbitration, more work was done in the peace effort than in any other
activity of the NCJW.

Arthur Brin was also an important leader in various groups
throughout the city. He was a member of the Anti-Defamation
Council of Minnesota and other Jewish welfare and refugee
groups. He worked with the Associated Jewish Charities of Minneapolis, the Community Chest and Council of Hennepin County,
the Council of Jewish Federation and Welfare Fund, and the Minneapolis Council of Social Agencies. As a member of B'nai B'rith,
he served as president of the Court, arbitration courts that were
used to settle minor squabbles.

The job for which Fanny had been molded by Nina Cohen in
her afternoon leadership studies was soon at hand. Her oratory
skills had been well developed since grade school, and her strong
personality and organizational ability made her a standout in any
group. Fanny felt it a particularly prestigious honor to be elected
president of the NCJW in 1932. Her election was a testament to

how successfully Eastern European Jews had adjusted to their new homeland. Because of her excellent work, Fanny was elected to a second term at the fourteenth annual national convention held in New Orleans, where she told her audience, "We believe that boundaries cannot be drawn satisfactorily with the sword."

In the late 1930s another cause took center stage in Fanny's life. There were many responses to Hitler's Nuremberg Laws of 1935, which deprived German Jews of various rights and forbade them to marry non-Jews. Some opted for quiet diplomacy; others demanded more dramatic action, including the easing of U.S. immigration restrictions. Fanny Brin and Charles Cooper, executive director of the Minneapolis Jewish Family Welfare Association, formed the Minneapolis Refugee Service Committee. By the fall of 1940, it had settled 250 European refugees in the city.

In 1944 Fanny organized the Women's United Nations Rally to promote peace and education. She was responsible for encouraging more than ten nondenominational women's organizations to participate in the rally. The rally was a great success and remains a yearly event to this day. (The theme of the Fifty-sixth United Nations Rally held in 2000 was "Global Peace." Fanny would have been heartbroken to know that peace had not yet been achieved by the turn of the twenty-first century, yet she would have been pleased to know that the cause, so near and dear to her heart, had not been abandoned.)

As horrible as the war was to Fanny and others fighting for world peace, there was even greater repulsion at the revelation that Jews by the millions had been exterminated by the Nazis. The guilt American Jews felt when they learned of this atrocity led many to support the movement called Zionism. Zionism emphasized creating a Jewish homeland, uniting the Jewish people, and bringing about a Hebrew cultural renaissance. It became a strong uniting factor for Jews of all backgrounds. Minnesota Zionists participated in the building of a Jewish state in Palestine by contributing to the Jewish National Fund and other social agencies that were working to help the Jews adjust to their new home. Fanny joined the cause and became a strong Zionist.

At the end of World War II, serious talk of establishing a United Nations dedicated to world peace was music to Fanny's ears. She had worked many years to further that cause and she was anxious that the idea move forward. The thrill of her life was attending the San Francisco United Nations Conference on International Organization. She would never forget her experiences there and the people she met. She compiled three notebooks while recording her days as a delegate and observer at the founding conference.

Although the war was over, the United Nations initiated, and the state of Israel formed, life was not easy for a Jew in Minneapolis. They still were excluded from many residential areas and were even barred from the Realty Board. They could not engage in certain professions, and Jewish physicians had trouble getting residencies. The Jews of Minneapolis rallied to the cause. Mount Sinai Hospital opened in 1951 and was the most modern hospital in the city. The seven-story institution answered the need for more hospital beds in the city, provided nonsectarian care, and offered a place for Jewish doctors to practice their profession.

Fanny's beloved Arthur died on November 5, 1947. A B'nai B'rith lodge in Minneapolis is named after him. Fanny was undaunted in her work and continued to take her civic responsibilities very seriously. She died on Monday, September 4, 1961, after a long illness, at seventy-six years of age. Her last hours were spent in Mount Sinai Hospital. Its national success was a tribute to the industry and capability of Minneapolis's Jewish community, of which Fanny and Arthur were so much a part. The *New York Times* carried her obituary.

At the time of her death, Fanny was honorary president of the Minneapolis chapter of the NCJW's International Relations and Peace Committee. She was member of the National Conference of Christians and Jews and the American Association of University Women. She had supported U.S. membership in the World Court and the United Nations. Fanny's son Howard married Ruth Firestone, daughter of Irma Cain Firestone, an activist in refugee resettlement work, president of the Saint Paul NCJW chapter, and Fanny's long-time friend. Ruth became a writer and activist herself.

All her life Fanny had fought for human rights and world peace. She did not let the restrictions imposed on women keep her from her civic duty. She urged all women to take their place in the world as leaders and educators. She had an undying faith in the belief that women could achieve greatness. Her own words speak volumes: "The need for women's participation grows daily. . . . I believe they can do more than they realize."

LENA O. SMITH

1885–1966

Civil Rights Advocate

*L*ena surveyed the Northwestern Building, where her real estate company was housed on the ground floor. After five successful years of selling homes, she had opened an office on Hennepin Street, but now she was getting out of the real estate business forever. Her working life was about to undergo a transformation, and there was much to do.

Lena was delighted to make the change. She was in a hurry to get on with the task at hand. Her clients John and Mary Parkinson needed her help. The elderly couple was being forced out of their home, the one they had lived in for twenty-five years. Not only had they made mortgage payments on the house, they had also made many improvements, including adding running water, indoor plumbing, lighting, a front porch, and a new roof. Lena felt the Parkinsons had been wronged in being forced out of their home, but she knew their case was not uncommon. White landowners often tried to renege on property deeds to black families, and they usually had the courts on their side.

But this was not to be the case today. For Lena O. Smith was taking down her real estate sign and putting up her attorney-at-law

WILLIAM MITCHELL COLLEGE OF LAW

Lena O. Smith

shingle. On June 27, 1921, Lena had been sworn into the Minnesota bar, and with that short ceremony, she passed into history as the first black woman attorney in Minneapolis. It had been a long struggle; she had worked hard to put herself through law school and to support her family, but her hardships had paid off. She filed her first lawsuit on behalf of the Parkinsons in the Minneapolis court system just eleven days after opening her practice. She won the discrimination case before a jury who saw justice served by awarding the Parkinsons the title of their home. John and Mary could now ease into old age knowing they could not be threatened by removal from their comfortable home ever again. Lena had prevented a serious injustice, and her fight to defend underrepresented and overburdened blacks in her city would be her mission for the rest of her life.

Lena was born on August 13, 1885, to John H. and Geneva D. Smith. She was the second of six children, four boys and two girls. Her first home was Lawrence, Kansas, a small community east of Topeka, just north of the Kansas River. The town boasted that it sat squarely between the Oregon and Santa Fe Trails, traveled by many settlers seeking their fortunes as they moved westward. Rugged individualism was a characteristic of the people of the town that had been founded on the political idea of "popular sovereignty." During the Civil War, Lawrence had been an important stop on the Underground Railroad, and many of its citizens had served as "conductors," secretly hiding runaway slaves until they could find safe passage to the North. The town had had to fight off proslavery attacks, the burning of homes and businesses—even the beautiful Eldridge Hotel—and the brutal killing of loved ones. Quantrill's Raid into Lawrence was one of the bloodiest episodes of the Civil War. Surrounded by Lawrence's long history of antislavery, Lena was exposed to the idea of equality and fairness for all people, black and white alike. (This "open" setting also played a part in the early life of writer Langston Hughes, who spent his formative years from 1902 to 1915 in Lawrence under the tutelage of his mother, who had grown up and attended school there.) Lena was to take these fundamental beliefs with her when, in 1905, she moved with her father to Iowa to find work to help support her mother and younger siblings, left behind in Kansas. They moved to a coal-mining town, Buxton, and Lena found a position in the company store. Her father's trade was printing, and perhaps this influenced Lena's developing talent for words and persuasion. Unfortunately, tragedy struck young Lena's life when her father died in 1906 of heart failure at the age of fifty-six. She moved with her family to Minneapolis and assumed the role of family protector and provider, having just turned twenty-one.

Lena had many talents and even more dreams. She took piano lessons and worked as a dramatic reader for the Chautauqua circuit, a very popular type of performance entertainment. Though it had originated near Chautauqua Lake in western New York, traveling companies now offered music, lectures, and short drama throughout the country. Lena loved the excitement of the tent programs and even took elocution lessons to improve her recitations. Minneapolis was an important town on many Chautauqua circuits. The schedule usually consisted of two performances a day for a weeklong engagement. Burly young "tent men" would erect huge canvas tents complete with lighting systems and dressing rooms for the performers. Lena was probably paid for her performances with a "season" ticket good for all the programs.

To earn a steady income, Lena began to work doing skin care from her home. But this occupation did not ease the young woman's restlessness. Feeling there was something else that she was called to do, Lena began to attend classes at the Barnes School of Sanitary Science and Embalming. She was the only woman and the only African American in her 1910 graduating class. Though Lena never officially worked as an embalmer, the skills she learned helped her get her next job as a beautician in downtown Minneapolis.

By 1913 Lena felt she had gained enough experience in hairdressing to branch out on her own. With another woman as a partner, she opened The Olive Hair Store on Nicollet Avenue in the heart of the city. Her establishment catered to the rich white women of Minneapolis. Her salon was lavishly decorated with velvet carpet and ostrich shades and equipped with manicure stations and massage beds. Lena advertised for clients in the newspaper and in local opera programs. But by the end of the year the salon was in trouble, and by 1914 Lena was forced to declare bankruptcy. No one could have convinced Lena at this low point in her career that there would be great fame and fortune for her in the future.

Race relations in the booming river town were beginning to feel the strain of a growing black population looking for opportunity and a dominant white citizenry determined not to offer it. In response to a nationwide concern about discrimination, Minneapolis formed a branch of the NAACP in 1914 to help fight for the equality of its black citizens. By this time Lena had moved on from the debacle of her hair salon business and had become a successful real estate broker. She was a pioneer in this high-profile industry, as most blacks were unjustly discouraged from the profession. The black newspaper in town acknowledged this novelty stating that Minneapolis was unique among cities having "a lady real estate dealer . . . in the person of Miss L. O. Smith."

Lena loved a challenge and she knew she had entered a profession where she would confront inequality and prejudice on a daily basis. Blacks were being shut out of white neighborhoods, and though the NAACP had won the *Buchanan v. Warley* case before the U. S. Supreme Court, the practice of segregation was still enforced by local authorities. Lena felt her clients, severely limited in the homes they were allowed to purchase, needed her expertise, but even she felt hindered at times. She constantly fought the restrictions imposed on black homebuyers and faced much of the hateful discrimination along with her clients. As fate would have it, her office was downstairs from the Northwestern College of Law, an independent school that offered night classes. Lena registered for her first law course in the fall of 1916. There were only three other women in her class of sixteen. It wasn't long before Lena began to direct her study toward segregation matters.

A fateful day of reckoning had arrived. Lena dressed carefully, straightened her hairdo, and walked out the door. She was headed down to Hennepin Avenue, but she was not going to work. She was going to the Pantages Theatre, a new vaudeville hall in the city's entertainment district, ironically situated on the same street as her real estate, and soon-to-be law, office. Owned by Greek immigrant Alexander Pantages, the establishment was number twenty-six of the 500 or so theaters that would open in the area. Only a few months old, the theater sparkled as the city's newest gem. It could hold 1,600 patrons and was the first theater to offer its guests the relief of air-conditioning. The marquee above the entrance of the two-story building was huge and inviting. Lena entered and stood in awe at the ceiling lavishly decorated with the intricacies of the Beaux Arts style. The gilded plaster ribbons, inset box seats, and tall, fluted columns were stunning, but she was not here to study architecture. Lena and the four black men with her had come with a purpose other than being entertained for the evening. The theater had a strict segregation policy. Lena and her accomplices headed away from the balcony slated for black seating and toward the "whites only" area. They were roughly refused admittance. This is what they expected, and their battle entered a new phase. Each of the four rejected patrons filed a legal suit, invoking Minnesota's law against discrimination in public accommodations. Lena also sued for assault. The black-owned *Twin City Star* applauded her action in its news columns and called on its readers to take businesses not offering equal treatment and facilities to court. Lena lost her suit, but the protests she initiated succeeded: A string of suits filed against the Pantages ended its segregated seating practices.

In April 1917 the United States entered the war in Europe. In part World War I was propelled by the belief that freedom for all people was a sacred right, which in turn bolstered the struggle by blacks for freedom and equality at home. Lena sadly waved good-bye as two of her brothers joined the army and went abroad. The flight of so many men overseas to fight the enemy left jobs open and homes vacant. Blacks and whites competed for both. Tension was rising despite pleas to lay domestic strife aside until after the war. By June 1918 membership in the Minneapolis NAACP had risen from 54 to 478, and Lena, her mother, and her sister were among the new registrants.

When the war was over and peace negotiated, eyes again turned toward racial injustice within the country. Returning black soldiers were victimized and lynchings increased; the irate black populace was ready to fight back. As an active member of the Executive Committee of the Minneapolis NAACP, Lena took her mission seriously. When news reached her organization of the lynching of three African-American men in Duluth by a rabble-rousing mob, the group went into action. Representatives immediately helped to establish a Duluth branch of the NAACP and sent back reports on the grand jury proceedings in the case. NAACP members raised money to help with court costs and to aid the families of the victims.

Lena had many successes, both financial and moral, during her fight for equality, but she was also an important presence on the black social scene in Minneapolis. One of her most cherished accomplishments was playing an influential role in her sister Frances's success. In 1920 she hosted Frances's debutante party. A rented hall was festively decorated with lanterns and flowers, and Frances looked lovely in pink and white. Lena looked around at the 150 guests in attendance listening to the live orchestra and felt that her family had come far since moving to Minneapolis. She felt as if all her sacrifices had paid off, not just for herself, but for those that were so dear to her heart. Frances would benefit from Lena's efforts and would make her sister proud. At the time of her debut, Frances was a freshman at the University of Minnesota; the next few years would bring her even greater success.

Still very active in the local NAACP, Lena became a member of the Legal Redress and Legislation Committee and began an investigation into some of the illegal practices that continued to deter many blacks from exercising free choice when it came to housing. The group uncovered a scheme by neighborhood home-owners to portray black families who were looking to buy homes in their area as opportunists trying to make a profit by pretending to want to buy in white neighborhoods in order to receive large monetary payoffs not to. The plan to rid white neighborhoods of black families failed to gather momentum. Lena and her mother were proof of that. They bought a house in a white neighborhood at 3905 Fourth Avenue South, a place they would call home until they died, a landmark the city would enter into its National Register of Historic Places in 1991.

Lena had already accomplished much in the fight for racial equality during the five years that she studied for the bar. She had taken a momentous stand at the Pantages Theatre, had become a vital member of the local NAACP, had joined the Women's Cooperative Alliance (WCA), had helped form a "Negro Council" to advance the African-American agenda of the WCA, and had chaired its law enforcement committee. She had also helped establish the

Business Women's Club, a primarily black organization, and was elected its first president. Lena was still called the real estate dealer, but this day would change all that. On June 16, 1921, thirty-five-year-old Lena Olive Smith became a member of the Minnesota bar. She was the first black woman in the state's history to achieve that distinction and one of only three in the entire country.

Lena had finally found her ultimate calling. She was successful from the first day she hung out her shingle. The Parkinsons and their case would never be forgotten, but they were only the first in a long string of clients.

Lena felt compelled to act in the face of racial inequality. She and other black leaders formed the Minneapolis branch of the National Urban League, an organization to help African Americans find housing and jobs. Lena was not exempt from discrimination. It saddened her to see her own brothers feel its scourge. Her oldest brother, Herman, had a good job as a porter on the Canadian National Railroad, but her three youngest brothers, John, Harold, and Prentiss, could not find regular work. They skipped from job to job, employed as hotel porters, stock boys, or in other low-status and low-paid positions.

Seeking to help people in the same situation as her brothers, Smith devoted most of her energy from that time forward to working with the NAACP and building a credible reputation for sound legal work. She became head of the Legal Redress Committee and served as the first woman president of the Minneapolis chapter from 1930 to 1939. She worked hard against discrimination of all kind in the areas of education, housing, public accommodations, the court system, and hate speech.

A new menace soon raised its ugly head in Lena's world—the Ku Klux Klan had formed a Minneapolis branch and its membership rolls were bulging. Thousands of people attended public meetings where D. W. Griffith's *Birth of a Nation*, a film steeped in a racist view of American history, was screened to promote the Klan's white-supremacy ideas. Lena and eight other community leaders met with the mayor on December 27, 1930, and were vehement in their demands that the movie be shut down. Mayor William F. Kunze agreed. Through various court maneuvers the theater managed to continue showing the film for a few days, before Lena went into action, calling on the NAACP to help with research to obtain information about cities where the film had incited riots or other trouble. By making this information known, Lena did her part to ensure that the theater was eventually barred from showing the film. Nearly ten years later, in 1940, Lena again worked hard to ban the film from Minnesota theaters. Meeting with the incumbent mayor, she and other leaders of the city were able to convince him that the film was an inexcusable affront to the black community. He agreed and threatened to revoke the theater's operating license. The theater acquiesced. On the national scene D. W. Griffith eventually apologized to the country for the film he had produced.

Lena had fought a valiant battle against discrimination. As she moved into her sixties, she took on fewer NAACP responsibilities, but she did not sit idle. She continued to contribute to her profession, serving on the bar association's Legislative Committee, the Public Relations Committee, and Special Committee on Civil Rights. She attended the inauguration of Lyndon Johnson in 1965 at the request of Hubert Humphrey.

Lena O. Smith was often called an aggressive, competent woman who wielded her power to help the unfortunate. She spoke tersely and often caught her adversaries off guard with her unconventional manner. Her many successes as a civil rights attorney were unprecedented for a lawyer (male or female) at that time. The *Minneapolis Spokesman* described her larger-than-life persona in glowing terms: "Minneapolis lawyers dread opposing Miss L. O. Smith."

LENA O. SMITH

Lena was a civic leader in her community, a civil rights activist, a successful attorney, and a faithful family supporter. She could not have been more proud than when her sister Frances graduated from the Minnesota College of Law, married a prominent doctor, and worked as a fund-raiser for the NAACP and the Urban League. Frances also helped with the integration of the YWCA, serving on its interracial committee. Both sisters were instrumental in mentoring young black women, holding meetings in their homes, and delivering lectures to eager audiences.

Lena's legacy lives on. Today the Minnesota's Black Women Lawyers Network honors her work with its Lena O. Smith Award for Courage and Achievement given to deserving women attorneys.

Lena was still practicing law in 1966, when she died at the age of eighty-one. She was thankful that she had lived long enough to see Congress pass the Civil Rights Act in 1964, but she knew there was still much work to be done. She had fought against injustice all her life, and though some things had changed, much remained the same. Nevertheless Lena was grateful for the full and rewarding life she had led. Concerning the conflict she encountered day in and day out, she once said, "Of course battles leave their scars, but I'm willing to make the sacrifice. I think it is my duty. It's a hard place to be—on the firing line—but I'm mighty glad I'm there."

Elizabeth Kenny
1880–1952

Innovator of Polio Treatments

*E*lizabeth was on her way to Minnesota deep in the mid-section of what was surely a vast and progressive country. Her trip to the United States had been lengthy and exhausting. Arriving in San Francisco with little Mary in hand, she went first to New York, then Chicago. Though she was armed with letters of intro-duction from doctors back home, Elizabeth's reception in the East had been very cool. Now mother and daughter were headed west again, with the expectation that the Mayo Clinic in Rochester, Minnesota, would extend a warm welcome. It did not. Elizabeth was sent on her way again; her final stop, and last hope, would be the University of Minnesota Medical School in Minneapolis. Elizabeth was disheartened by the rejection she had experienced, but she also felt she had an important mission in life, and so she pushed herself to meet with still more doctors. The doctors from the university medical school asked Elizabeth to demonstrate her techniques on some of the patients they had in the ward, and Eliz-abeth was happy to do so. She approached one of the patients in the hospital bed and spoke in a calming voice. She laid hot, moist packs on the spastic muscles and began to stretch them out. Elizabeth knew this was her last chance to impress the American doctors, and she was afraid they would not respond favorably. She worked on several patients, nursing them with all the skills she knew, and then she stepped aside and held her breath. The renowned physicians observing her work had been very quiet. But the head of orthopedics, with true midwestern stoicism, said simply, "I think you had better stick around for a while." She did.

It was 1940, and Minneapolis would become her home and the city where she and other colleagues would pioneer her new treatment for victims of polio, a disease that was affecting millions of people, including the U.S. president, Franklin D. Roosevelt.

Elizabeth Kenny was born on September 20, 1880, in Warialda, New South Wales, Australia. Her parents, Michael Kenny and Mary Moore Kenny, were homesteaders who moved around the country fairly often. Elizabeth was a tough kid, and when she was eight, she broke her arm. Dr. Aeneas McDonnell was called to set the broken bone, and in him Elizabeth found a lifelong role model to nourish her caring spirit. She was rarely in school, yet she had a thirst for knowledge that would not be quenched by the hard life that outback settlers lived.

Elizabeth taught herself to read, and at the age of sixteen she graduated from St. Ursula's College. As a young girl, committed to helping her frail brother get strong and able, she began to study physiology and anatomy at a private hospital. Her brother William became her first patient as she guided him through many hours of calisthenics to build his bones and muscles.

Elizabeth was a strong-willed girl, and the nursing profession suited her determined character. She began to provide care to rural bush families free of charge. Sometimes she would sit in the sidecar of a friend's motorcycle, flying through the wilds of the outback over a 10-square-mile territory. Mostly, though, she rode on

LIBRARY OF CONGRESS, LC-USZ62-119197

Elizabeth Kenny, waving from the Queen Mary

horseback, and cowboys galloping across the bush to find a nurse would direct her to the sparsely situated homes where families needed care. She usually tended to accident victims, sick children, and mothers giving birth. But one day in 1910, in the northeast Australia bush territory, she came upon a unique case. Three-year-old Amy McNeil was in great pain. Elizabeth noticed that her leg was contracted in a strange position. When she tried to straighten the leg, the child screamed out and the limb immediately folded up again. Not knowing what to do, she rode 2 miles to telegraph her friend and mentor Dr. McDonnell, who was practicing more than a 100 miles away. The Toowoomba doctor diagnosed the child as having infantile paralysis but sadly noted that there was nothing to do for the debilitating condition. Elizabeth was directed by telegram to "do the best you can for the symptoms."

Infantile paralysis or poliomyelitis, first identified by a British physician in 1789 and later reported in 1840 by a German doctor, became the plague of the twentieth century. In 1887 there had been an outbreak in Sweden; the first sign of polio in the United States was in Vermont in 1894, affecting 134 victims. But that was just the beginning of the havoc wrought by this dreadful disease. In 1916 over 9,000 cases had been reported in New York City. Although the disease attacked mostly children, Franklin Roosevelt had contracted the disease in 1921, as a young man, in the Bay of Bundy, Canada. In the coming years the condition would simply be called polio, and the numbers of affected children would soar. Parents would live in fear every summer—the season of the greatest number of outbreaks—that the devastating disease would strike their family. Children were prevented from going to the beach or swimming in any pools because there was some thought that the disease was spread by water. Each year the number of those suffering from polio rose, and in 1934 Los Angeles reported nearly 2,500 cases in just one hospital. Through most of this time the cause of the disease was unknown, and there was little treatment and no cure. In 1928 American Philip Drinker invented a large metal tank, called the "iron lung," to help victims who were experiencing complicated respiratory problems. The lung, along with the "rocking bed," crutches, and metal braces, alleviated some of the effects of polio. Elizabeth wanted to do something to, first, relieve the child's pain, and, second, prevent the paralysis from occurring in the first place.

Relying on her past observations of Aborigines who soothed pain with heat treatments, she tried a few remedies, such as a heated salt bag that was too heavy and a hot poultice that was too sticky and incapable of holding the required level of heat long enough to relieve young Amy's pain. Finally Elizabeth spied an old blanket in the home. She picked it up and immediately tore it to shreds. She dropped the pieces into boiling water and wrung them out, then she wrapped the girl's contracted limbs in the hot woolen strips. The heat seemed to relieve some of the child's pain and she fell asleep. Elizabeth was called away to another ranch, but she instructed Amy's mother to continue with the steaming rags. By the next week, the child was free of pain, but it seemed she could not use the muscles in her leg. Elizabeth devised a unique plan of treatment and began to move and exercise the paralyzed limbs, reeducating them how to function properly. Eventually Amy was able to move the affected muscles by herself. Elizabeth treated five other cases in the same way with the same startling results.

When Dr. McDonnell found out that her polio patients were all doing well, he knew Elizabeth had made a startling discovery. He prophesied great achievement in the fight against polio for the young woman, but Elizabeth was more concerned with the here and now. Despite the satisfaction she felt helping children afflicted with polio, Elizabeth's life had taken a sad turn. With all the medical skill she possessed, Elizabeth could not save her father, who died in 1913. Her mother sold the family farm and moved into a small house in town.

Eager to become an officially licensed nurse, Elizabeth joined the Australian Army Nursing Service in 1915. She worked on carrier ships, often in dangerous waters, to help wounded soldiers returning home from the war. After a year of service, she was promoted from staff nurse to the rank of sister, a Nurse Corps title roughly equivalent to first lieutenant. On the front in France, Elizabeth was shot and took shrapnel in one of her legs. Sister Kenny served for three years in the medical corps and was awarded a British War Medal. After her discharge she returned to helping poor Aborigine families of the Australian bush country.

She busied herself again with helping develop a treatment for polio victims. Not much had happened in the past few years, and the standard treatment for patients was still to immobilize the contracting limbs using splints or plaster casts. Sister Kenny thought this treatment was barbaric. With her hot-pack treatments, her patients had experienced a lessening of pain and eventually gained some use of the distorted limbs. Elizabeth was a compassionate nurse, and in 1926 she developed a rigid stretcher that would minimize the jolting of patients who often went into shock as they were moved through rough bush terrain to reach local hospitals. She was astute enough a businesswoman to patent her invention, and she sold distribution rights throughout the world. Her "Sylvia" stretcher was so successful that she was able to travel and do charity nursing for many years on its royalties.

The year 1926 was also important personally for Elizabeth. She had met an eight-year-old orphan who won her heart. Elizabeth adopted the girl and named her Mary Stewart. She was the first single, unwed woman in Queensland to be allowed to adopt a child. Mary would later train as a Kenny therapist and carry on the work of her famous mother.

Elizabeth was building a good reputation among polio patients with her unconventional methods of treatment. She opened a ramshackle clinic in Townsville, setting up beds for patients under an awning. Her makeshift clinic eventually received government status, and its success enabled her to establish eight other such clinics in several rural towns. The clinics were run by Kenny therapists whom Elizabeth trained. Her nontraditional ideas, however, were not well accepted by the medical community. She was called "quack" by some and refused hospital privileges by most.

But stories of her successful treatments were spreading across the globe. She would persevere in trying to get influential doctors to consider her course of action, and in 1937 she was successful in opening a clinic in the wing of Queen Mary's Hospital for Children in Carshalton, Surrey, England. She published "Infantile Paralysis and Cerebral Diplegia," an article that foreshadowed a textbook. That same year President Roosevelt announced the establishment of the National Foundation for Infantile Paralysis. This brought even more attention to the work being done by the medical profession to treat polio victims.

By 1940 Sister Kenny knew the time was right to visit the United States. Doctors in the States were more aggressive in treating polio than those in the rest of the world, and Americans were willing to sacrifice their time and hard-earned money to arrest the disease. Eddie Cantor, a famous entertainer, had used the slogan "March of Dimes" when he pleaded for radio listeners to send their loose change to the National Foundation for Infantile Paralysis to help in the fight against polio. This annual fund-raising campaign had been very successful, and the foundation had supplied the initial funding needed to keep Sister Kenny in Minneapolis and to conduct a study of her methods. The National Foundation endorsed her course of treatment in an article in the prestigious *Journal of the American Medical Association,* and a medical rev-

ELIZABETH KENNY

olution followed. Doctors abandoned splints and casts in the treatment of polio victims and began applying hot packs and muscle rehabilitation procedures.

Sister Kenny began her work in the United States managing a ward at the Minneapolis General Hospital, a complex of modern brick buildings that had updated the 1887 original structure. General Hospital served the community, including those patients who could not afford to pay for medical services. Sister Kenny became nationally famous for her innovations in nursing care, and polio sufferers from across the country flocked to Minneapolis for her treatment. In 1942 the Lymanhurst School-Hospital, a branch of General Hospital, became the Sister Elizabeth Kenny Institute. An eight-story annex was added to accommodate two elevators big enough to hold the thirty iron lungs in constant demand and the nearly fifty patients who were admitted each day. The hospital grew in later years to be a major rehabilitation facility for those suffering from any crippling accident or disease.

Elizabeth's life was rich and full. Her career had been solidified in Minnesota, and her reputation had spread around the world. And now the Australian bush nurse without any formal medical education was invited to visit the White House. She was to meet with President Roosevelt, himself a victim of polio. It was a warm day in June 1943 when she walked up the steps of the Capitol of the nation that had accepted her and her radical polio treatments. It certainly was a country of opportunity.

A year later Elizabeth was recognized by the *New York Sun* as the "Outstanding Woman of the Year." From 1943 to 1951 the Gallup Poll named her the second most admired woman in America; Eleanor Roosevelt was first. One of the highlights of her career was the invitation she received in 1947 for a private audience with Pope Pius XII. The thrill of that event was unparalleled. When the Holy Father presented her with a medal of the Holy Family for her efforts in helping the children of the world, she knew she was indeed blessed. She would carry that papal medal with her for the rest of her life. In 1951 she was given another honor when she became the only woman ever to receive the rare U.S. Joint Congressional Committee award of "Visa and Free Passage across the Borders of the United States of America." After publishing her third textbook, *The Kenny Concept of Infantile Paralysis and Its Treatment*, she was awarded honorary degrees by Rochester University, Rutgers University, and New York University. By 1952 she was at the height of her career, she had moved up the final notch on the Gallup Poll and stood above all other women of her time; she was number one on the list of the public's most admired women.

On the outside Elizabeth was an imposing figure. She often intimidated members of the medical profession with her stubbornness and authoritative manner, but she was always kind and gentle toward her patients. One of her patients characterized her as a woman who "inspired confidence just by her manner and the way she carried herself." She was a tall, sturdy woman who often wore long black dresses and no jewelry. She would spice up her attire by wearing the broad hats of the era, ostrich feathers and all. She didn't wear makeup; her intense eyes didn't need any help to get your attention. Her strong Australian accent was certainly in contrast to the sharp Minnesotan speech of America's Midwest. On the inside Elizabeth had the courage of her convictions and would not back down when she thought she was right. Though the pervading medical thinking of the time was that the disease attacked the spinal cord nerve centers, causing the paralysis of limbs, Elizabeth thought otherwise. She had seen spasms in the muscles before paralysis set in. If this were the case, she argued, the virus would have to be in the bloodstream. Could not a vaccine kill the virus if it were in the blood?

Doctors and scientists devoted much time and effort furiously trying to find a way to end the epidemic. Funding for the project was helped by the March of Dimes campaign, which was a huge success. Donations poured in from across the country. Each poster child was a constant reminder of the harsh effects of the disease. People gave generously, either hoping that a cure would be found in time to help their afflicted child or grateful that their family had not yet fallen victim to its torment. Funding from the Kenny Institute and the World Health Organization were also major contributors to polio research.

But the epidemic raged on. In 1945, after the end of World War II, the country saw more than 20,000 cases a year. Help arrived in the person of Dr. Jonas Salk, the son of Russian-Jewish immigrants, the first in his family to attend college. After medical school Salk accepted a position at a Pittsburgh lab and began working with the National Foundation. He was awarded a research grant and launched his eight-year journey to find a polio vaccine. By 1952 the United States reported 58,000 cases of polio, the most ever in one year. Patients at the Kenny Institute were described as "stacked up like cord wood." Time was running out for many children, and Salk and his lab staff worked long and hard to develop a vaccine.

Finally, in 1953 Dr. Jonas Salk succeeded in producing a polio vaccine that could be administered by inoculation, and some initial trials were begun. On April 12, 1955, his discovery was made public. Within a short time a million school children received a polio vaccine shot. After just three years of inoculations, there were fewer than 200 cases of the disease in the United States. Dr. Salk was hailed as a miracle worker by a grateful country. Soon after Salk's discovery, Dr. Albert Sabin announced a live virus vaccine that could be taken orally. Lines of children filled school yards across the nation to receive their polio vaccine sugar cube. The epidemic screeched to a halt, and the disease was virtually eradicated overnight.

Elizabeth did not live to see the demise of the dreaded disease. She died on November 30, 1952, after returning to Australia the year before. She knew her end was near and was happy that she had accomplished so much. She cherished the messages she had received from grateful parents and patients over the years. After all, helping the children was the end that justified the means. She would have been so proud not only of Dr. Salk's accomplishment in finding a vaccine, but also of the fact that he refused to patent it; he did not want to profit from his discovery. He, like Sister Kenny, just wanted to see the disease wiped out.

Sister Kenny's story would live on. RKO Pictures made a film of her life, starring Rosalind Russell who was, coincidentally, a Sister Elizabeth Kenny Institute board member. Russell received a Best Actress nomination for her role portraying Sister Kenny. The Elizabeth Kenny Institute, founded in 1942 in Minneapolis, flourished, and after the epidemic was over, it grew to become a major rehabilitation facility for those suffering as a result of crippling injuries or diseases. Today it is part of the Abbott Northwestern Hospital complex.

Although desperately ill, Elizabeth finished her work, *My Battle and Victory*, which was published posthumously in 1955. This work followed her autobiography, *And They Shall Walk*, and three textbooks on her methods. She bequeathed her Florence Nightingale desk and her Book of Common Prayer to the United Nations. The Sister Kenny Memorial Fund in Australia still brings in more than $1.5 million to help rural and remote nurses.

Bush nurse Elizabeth Kenny had persevered in the face of great obstacles presented by highly educated and well-practiced doctors of her time. Once accepted, her methods were used for fifteen years on tens of thousands of victims. The healthy and productive lives of the children who received Sister Kenny's hot packs and muscle-stretching exercises have been documented by three survivors in an oral history entitled "Polio's Legacy." Some of the survivors even became doctors themselves, a testament to the extraordinary gift Sister Kenny gave to the children of the world.

BLANCHE YURKA

1887–1974

Star of Stage and Screen

*T*he majestic wooden columns had been polished and waxed to perfection. The elegant glass chandeliers had been dusted, and Giovanni Battista Smeraldi's artistry glistened in the sparkling shadows of incandescent candlelight. The Italian painter had worked on several palaces in the Vatican, and his accomplishments here in this luxurious hotel were no less grand. The ornate silverware and crystal goblets had been set carefully on tables dressed in starched white linens. Built in 1923 when money was rolling in, the Biltmore Hotel, a landmark of Spanish-Italian Renaissance architecture, had survived the Depression and once again symbolized the luxurious lifestyle for which Hollywood was known. The mention of its name connoted elegance and opulence. The area called the Biltmore Bowl was made up of several rooms, the most prestigious of these being the Crystal Ballroom, with its graceful arches and small inset balconies. In 1927 Mary Pickford, Douglas Fairbanks, Louis B. Mayer, and other important movie industry moguls had sat in this very room to form the organization that came to be known simply as the Academy. It was here at one of the

small tables where the design for the much-sought-after statuette—
later to be called, familiarly, Oscar—was sketched on a dinner
napkin.

All was set for the night's spectacular event, the Academy of
Motion Picture Arts and Sciences banquet where the Academy
Awards for 1936 would be presented. The gala evening would be
broadcast live over the radio to the entire country. Blanche stepped
onto the graceful staircase leading toward the Crystal Ballroom.
She found her place and settled into her chair, ready for the festivities to begin. She had certainly come a long way from singing
"Forsaken, forsaken, forsaken, am I" in the kitchen of her family's
little shack, the "baracek" in Saint Paul, Minnesota. She had been
magnanimously lauded for her role in *A Tale of Two Cities*, one of the
spectacular films nominated tonight for Best Picture. Who would
have thought that the woman once called the "Bohemian Girl"
would find herself surrounded by the grandeur of the Academy
Award night ceremonies, listening to George Jessel entertain such
stars as Gary Cooper, William Powell, Spencer Tracy, Norma
Shearer, and Carole Lombard. It was a night Blanche would remember every detail of for the rest of her life.

Blanche Yurka was born on a sunny Sunday morning, June 18,
1887, in Saint Paul, Minnesota, to Anton and Caroline Jurka, who
later changed their name to Yurka. Her parents had originally emigrated from what would become Czechoslovakia, and like many
other Czechs of Minnesota they had kept their children interested
in the culture of their forebears, establishing orchestras for music
education and theatrical companies for the production of many
native plays. Blanche's father had worked as a newspaper reporter
on a Czech paper in Chicago after he emigrated at the age of
twenty-eight. When he heard of an opening for a Czech teacher at

MINNEAPOLIS STAR-JOURNAL, MINNESOTA HISTORICAL SOCIETY

Blanche Yurka appearing with the Bainbridge Players in "Candida"

the Jefferson School in Saint Paul to teach the children of Bohemian parents, he grabbed the opportunity, though the pay was poor indeed. Anton became a well-known educator in Saint Paul for his untraditional teaching methods. Devoted to his music, he began and ended each school day with a musical interlude. He also regarded exercise as a worthy endeavor, so a portion of each day was spent doing some sort of physical activity. Blanche was delighted when she learned that her father had harbored a secret desire to be an actor. He'd told young Blanche that he had wanted to go on the stage when he was a boy, but his family had considered this a worthless ambition and he was forced to give up his dream. Amateur acting, however, was one of his chief pastimes.

Blanche was happy in Saint Paul. Her childhood was spent with loving parents and four siblings, Charlie, Tom, Rose, and Mila, in the little cottage with a nice garden. She loved to suck on icy apples from the old wooden barrel in the storeroom. A creative child, she would entertain her brother Tom with stories as they sat warming their faces in front of the big iron stove while their backsides froze in the cold parlor air. She didn't like having to speak Czech at the dinner table, but years later she counted the sounds of her parents' native language as among the most pleasurable and affectionate of familiar sounds. She and sister Rose would sing together after supper as they washed the dishes. She loved the smell of *kolacky*, sweet turnovers filled with citron and other fruit. Most Czechs in Saint Paul had to raise their own poppies in order to harvest the poppy seeds needed to make this homeland delicacy, but they were a must-have dessert for religious festivals. The family was poor, but there was plenty to do. Often an insignificant event was the cause of great excitement. The day the small bathroom was installed in her home was a childhood memory never to be forgotten. Blanche was to write much later, "We managed to do a lot of living in those few little rooms."

In the fall of 1900, her comfortable Minnesota home was only a distant memory. Her father had taken a job in New York City, where he hoped he could make a better living. He moved his family to a cheap railroad flat apartment. The quarters were small; Blanche's sister Mila slept on a couch in the dining room. Their furniture had been sold in Saint Paul, and now most of what they had was makeshift and homemade. Because Blanche was too young to enter high school, though she had finished grade school before the move, it was decided she would repeat eighth grade. One of the bright spots in a dull academic year was her singing lessons with the musical director of the Czech singing society. She was delighted when she was chosen to play the prima donna role, and how ironic it seemed that her singing debut would be in the opera by Balfe, *Bohemian Girl*, performed in Czech.

Blanche's family was extremely poor, and the entertainment she found for herself in New York theaters required her to walk long distances, sometimes 50 or more blocks from Wadleigh High School, in order to save on carfare so she could afford the meager admission price to the topmost gallery. At this time Broadway was a glorious and inviting row of playhouses from the Star Theater on Thirteenth Street to the New York Theater on Forty-fifth Street. And Blanche wanted to enjoy every production put on in every one of them. School became a struggle for Blanche. Her mother had hopes of her being a schoolteacher like her father and her sister Mila, but those dreams were dashed when good grades seemed impossible. Blanche liked English and French, but she soon began to hate school. Math and physics were impossible for the "prima donna" whose head had already been turned in the direction of the theater world.

Through a near miracle of being in the right place at the right time, a unique audition, and her father's facility with the German language, Blanche was awarded a scholarship to a new school headed by Heinrich Conried, impresario of the Metropolitan Opera House (the Met). Blanche was relieved to give up school and devote the next two years to singing. Her world consisted of tough lessons, daily scales, and even German lessons because her teacher spoke no English, but despite the hard work, it was paradise for young Blanche. She attended the rehearsals and performances of great vocalists and came in contact with famous singers such as Enrico Caruso, Antonio Scotti, and Olive Fremstad.

But as much as Blanche loved her life, things were not going well for her. She loved to sing, anytime, anywhere, and she involved herself in all sorts of creative projects. She could not turn down an offer to perform. During a rehearsal for a performance not connected with the Met, Blanche, sick with a cold, refused to step out of the role, her voice ultimately failed, and her vocal chords were severely damaged. Her Met teachers, unaware of her outside activities, were puzzled over the troubles with her voice, but there was nothing to be done. Her scholarship was discontinued. Blanche was out of the Met and all that it had offered.

She spent weeks mourning the life she had lost. But the dark despair of having failed vanished when she was accepted into the newly organized Institute for Musical Art, now the famed Juilliard School of Music. As she explained in her autobiography, "I was to be given another chance and every possible opportunity to nurse the strained vocal chords back to normal." She worked hard at her disciplined routine, and two years nearly flew by. Then disaster struck again. During an exam performance, Blanche felt her throat tighten as she approached a B-flat at the end of an aria. Her voice cracked and she had never felt so terrible. She ran home in disgrace, a failure, but there was more to it than that. Blanche realized that she would never be able to sing, that the "sick agony of fright would always haunt me." In the director's office a few days later, Dr. Frank Damrosch suggested that Blanche take her obvious dramatic flair and look toward a career on the stage, but Blanche had no intention of doing that.

After weeks of disappointment, though she was still living at home, Blanche knew she had to find some way to make a living. Her singing career was virtually over, so she began to wonder how one would get started acting in the theater. Her first plan involved sitting, morning to evening, for several months, on a second-rate theatrical agent's office bench hoping for a bit part in a road show. Though she was not working, she was busy watching and learning. She studied the work of actors she admired, sneaking into theater matinees to watch them. She decided to change her tactics and gave up her bench in the agent's outer office. She marched herself down to the Met and asked to see her old mentor, Mr. Conried. She told him of her plans to work on the stage and left his office with a recommendation in hand. She added a personal note to Mr. Conried's letter and sent both off to David Belasco of the Belasco Theatre. Belasco, dubbed "The Bishop of Broadway" because of his habit of wearing the collar and dress of a cleric, lived in an apartment over his Broadway theater offices. For nearly twenty years a Belasco play would open in the fall, run all season, and then go on a sold-out tour for the next season. Blanche was playing the long shot. When an envelope arrived from Belasco's office, Blanche was excited; she had been summoned! She was asked a battery of questions by his secretary and told to await word from the mighty Belasco. When word finally came, Blanche donned her one and only black dress for evening wear, grabbed her sister Mila's hand, and raced down to the theater. Meeting Belasco was a dream come true for the now aspiring actress, and when he asked her to prepare one or two audition scenes for him, she jumped to the task. Eventually she signed a contract with his company for the upcoming season; she would be paid $25 a week to be a general understudy.

The world was again opening up for Blanche. One of her earliest acquaintances in the theater was a slim, beguiling actress and leader of the chorus, soon to be off to Hollywood, Katharine Hepburn. And not long after that Blanche found herself making close friends with the young actress playing General Warren's little daughter in *The Warrens of Virginia*, Mary Pickford. Blanche learned a lot from Mary, already an accomplished actress at sixteen. Sharing dressing rooms, doubling up on hotel rooms to save money, eating on a shoestring, the girls were inseparable. When the play's run ended, Mary, in need of money to support her family went to work for $5.00 a day in a dingy studio on West Fourteenth Street where D. W. Griffith was experimenting with "motion pictures." She had been embarrassed to tell her stage friends at Belasco's that she was selling out to the movies, but as Blanche sat to watch her work, she realized that Mary's petite size and irresistible charm were well suited to the new medium. "America's Sweetheart" would soon take Hollywood by storm.

The skies were darkening and war was raging in Europe. Blanche was struggling in her career but felt she had to help the war effort somehow and soon became involved in playing benefits and working for the Stage Women's War Relief. Still she could not blame the war for her sputtering career. She had had some high points, even some starring roles here and there, but she never seemed able to sustain success for any length of time.

But the sun was to shine for Blanche once again when she was chosen to play the leading role of Gina, the mother, in Henrik Ibsen's *The Wild Duck* to be produced by the Actors' Theatre. Blanche threw herself into the part and even helped rework some of her character's speeches to make them seem more believable. She found that the part called for her to draw upon inspiration from her own mother, her *maminka*, whom she had often described as a "giver" in the world. She wrote in her autobiography, "For mother, too, was one of those earthy indispensable members of the human race. So completely was Gina my mother that often I would say to her, 'Well, Maminka, you gave a good performance tonight.' " Her work was applauded by critics; one wrote, "But the best performance is probably that of Blanche Yurka as the patient, ageless Gina. It dominates the whole piece, even in the moments when she is not on stage."

Things were going well for Blanche at last, and she was able to direct some of her energies toward her private life. While acting in her next play, *The Lawbreaker*, though not a box office success, Blanche achieved a little personal success of her own. She met charming and talented Ian Keith, who was working in another play. Their fourteen-month courtship was great fun. Blanche and Ian attended theater matinees, dined together daily, and planned a future playing great theatrical couples. When they decided to marry, they headed to a little church in Chicago, where Blanche had joined Ian during the run of his new play. They honeymooned at the Edgewater Beach Hotel overlooking scenic Lake Michigan, swam in the lake's brisk waters, and played a little golf. Their carefree times together were short-lived, however, and amid career jealousy and an uncertain future, the two were soon divorced.

Blanche plunged herself into the hectic life of the Roaring Twenties. She reveled in her success as the Spanish mother who harbors a young gypsy girl in *The Squall*, meeting such celebrities as Charlie Chaplin, Paul Reynaud, and Charles Hanson Towne. The play was to run for two years, first on Broadway, then on tour. Blanche finally felt she was able to relax a little. She had made a name for herself, one that had been up in the lights of Broadway. She had more money than she had ever had before; with a little planning she should be set for life. Blanche's brother Charlie helped her invest in real estate, the "safe" place for her money, he said. Here it would be shielded from the volatility of the stock market. Unfortunately, it wasn't.

Blanche was able to enjoy two major successes before the carefree era of the Roaring Twenties came to an abrupt halt. She often thought about how far she had come in so little time and how bumpy the road from Saint Paul to New York had been. When an offer came to go to Minneapolis to star in a season of Ibsen, Blanche felt it was time to go home. She starred in *The Wild Duck*, and then tackled *Hedda Gabler*, *The Lady from the Sea*, and *A Doll's House*. Her work in Minnesota was like a rebirth for Blanche. She was hailed for her performance in every play, but more than that, this engagement was "to prove a preparation for one of my greatest adventures in acting." Once again Minnesota had fueled the career of Blanche Yurka.

On returning to New York, Blanche was thrilled to star again as Gina in *The Wild Duck* in a production at the Forty-ninth Street Theatre on Broadway. She also agreed to assemble the cast and direct the play as well. When the curtain went up on November 19, 1928, only two weeks after she signed the contract, Blanche's work was acclaimed by the critics, but there was a storm gathering on the horizon.

The Great Depression saw the number of plays produced fall significantly, from 233 productions in the 1929–30 season to just 187 the next year. This trend would continue for some time, hitting a low of only 98 shows in 1939. Many of Broadway's talented actresses and actors left for better opportunities offered by Hollywood. The film industry was not as hard-hit. The public, it seemed was willing to spend its hard-earned nickels and dimes to escape into a movie theater for an hour or so.

Blanche was satisfied with her life in the theater, but she was very excited when her agent arranged an audition for her in an upcoming movie, *A Tale of Two Cities*, set during the French Revolution, to be produced by David O. Selznick. In a New York screen test, she stunned the test director and received Selznick's approval.

Blanche felt herself very lucky; more than sixty actresses had tried out for the enviable role of Dickens's Madame Defarge. She boarded her first ever cross-country airplane flight and headed to the MGM Studio in Hollywood. Her screen debut as the cackling, evil Defarge was unforgettable. The film was nominated for Best Picture in 1936. (The award went to *The Great Ziegfeld*.)

Following the success of *A Tale of Two Cities*, Blanche signed a contract to tour the country in a one-woman show. She was excited by the challenge and created a unique show in which she could present her lectures on theater performance techniques as well as recreate some of her more famous dramatic scenes. Once again her career was changing direction, and her performance in her first show, "The Ever Expanding Theatre," at the University of Minnesota saw Blanche again connect with her Saint Paul–Minneapolis roots. Commenting on the lecture she had given to several thousand students, she wrote to her sister Rose, "The lecture was broadcast in both St. Paul and Minneapolis. . . . The whole thing was a far cry from the performances of the yellow-haired youngster who used to stand on the teacher's platform in Jefferson school in St. Paul singing for an occasional visitor." Fewer tickets were sold the second night when she would be performing her second show, "Arc of the Theatre," because Franklin Roosevelt was speaking on the Capitol steps in Saint Paul, but she was okay with that; after all he was speaking for free. But James Gray of the *St. Paul Pioneer Press* wrote of her performance, "Resolution, imagination and a real creative vitality are in command." Blanche was happy to be invited back three more times. She was also delighted to learn that her old friend Tyrone Guthrie was starting a theater in Minneapolis, which was becoming the cultural center of the state of which Blanche called herself "a native daughter."

Once back in Minnesota, Blanche could not resist a pilgrimage to the small cottage where she had enjoyed her youth. She crossed the Mississippi River and recalled to Rose, "Old Man River is as impressive as ever, but, oh, the little house looks very shabby indeed, and so small!"

By 1955, after a few more years on Broadway, Blanche decided to retire from the stage. The *New York Times* printed her "farewell" letter to Broadway. Not long after that, she was approached by Prentice Hall to write a book about the theater. Her book would be based on her experiences in the theater and her impressions of Broadway. *Dear Audience: A Guide to the Enjoyment of the Theatre* got good reviews, though it was not a resounding success. The December 10, 1959, *New York Telegraph* called it "a beguiling and entrancing introduction to playgoing." Later, still touring the lecture circuit, she recorded her "one-woman" programs for Folkways Records.

Blanche did not completely retire from the theater after all; she had one more run at Broadway stardom. She played a small but noteworthy part in the successful *Dinner at Eight*, which opened at the Alvin Theatre and ran from September 27, 1966, to January 14, 1967, for a total of 127 performances.

Throughout the years she had worked in many entertainment media. She had dabbled in opera, delighted audiences on Broadway, entertained moviegoers in more than twenty films, recorded her live performances for radio buffs, and she entered the newest medium, television, when the nine-member cast of *Dinner at Eight* were guests on *What's My Line?* She would also go on to appear in numerous *Kraft Television Theatre* episodes. And 1966–67 was a good year for Blanche in other ways too. During the run of *Dinner at Eight*, she found time to finish her autobiography, *Bohemian Girl: Blanche Yurka's Theatrical Life*, as well as give acting lessons to aspiring young thespians in the bedroom left vacant after her sister Rose's heartbreaking death. At this time she was unanimously awarded the first honorary life membership on the Actors' Equity Council as a celebration of her long and distinguished career. When she was awarded a doctor of humane letters by the University of Tampa, Blanche came to think back on how her mother had regretted her leaving school, dashing all hopes of her becoming a schoolteacher. Now here she was, sitting on a university dais having the extraordinary honor of a college degree bestowed upon her.

Ever the restless soul, Blanche Yurka reached the culmination of her theatrical career in a personal triumph when she was featured in *The Madwoman of Chaillot*, produced in London in 1970. Blanche was eighty-three years old.

Blanche died four years later, on June 6, 1974, of arteriosclerosis. Her career was stellar, and her legacy survives in the recordings of her work, her books, and the more than twenty films in which she appeared. She lives on forever in the hearts and souls of moviegoers everywhere. The words of one of her reviewers captures her essence as a stage and film star: "Blanche Yurka has a voice that ripples on like globules of silver, or—say—moonlight on water. . . . She is worth dozens of revolving stages, and scores of scenes. Here was the supreme historic achievement of the performance."

MAUD HART LOVELACE
1892–1980

A True Minnesota Novelist

*M*aud was beginning to wonder what she was doing spending the winter in sunny California, so far from her home in Minnesota. She had left her first semester studies at the University of Minnesota to visit her grandmother. Also, she hoped to rest and fully recover from an operation to remove her appendix. But she didn't want to relax completely; she was determined to work on her writing career while here. Despite the great excitement on the West Coast, as aviators took off in seaplanes over the Pacific and influential businesspeople began planning for the upcoming Panama-California Exposition, Maud longed for home and knew she was a Minnesotan at heart. Despite the miles, she still felt connected to her hometown of Mankato, where luscious green hills had dominated her landscape ever since she could remember. In her mind's eye she could see her whole town, the Pleasant Grove School, her home at 333 Center Street, shady Sibley Park, and the Minnesota River as it flowed through the deep valley that she loved. But her carefree days of running the grassy hills and catching fireflies were coming to an end. She was a young woman now, on the edge of great adventure. Seeing roses bloom in December,

GENE GARRETT, MINNESOTA HISTORICAL SOCIETY

Maud Hart Lovelace

whereas back home everything would be covered with freezing snow, started her creativity flowing. She began to write and write and sent her stories out to various publications. She expected an acceptance letter at any time, but the days passed one after the other and nothing happened. No one seemed interested in her stories.

Her mother's brother, Uncle Frank, was ranching not far from San Diego, and he thought he had a possible solution. He brought over a typewriter and explained to Maud that she should type her stories instead of hand writing them. Maud was willing to try anything. She typed out a story, titled it "Number Eight," and sent it off to the *Los Angeles Times Sunday Magazine.* Then, again, she waited. Her high hopes were soon dashed. Still she bought the *Times* every weekend, scanning the literary section for clues on how to improve her writing and increase the chances of getting her stories accepted. Then one day, as Maud leafed through the *Sunday Magazine,* she stopped dead still. Her heart began to race. There before her eyes, in the prestigious *Los Angeles Times,* was her story "Number Eight." Her work was finally in print. She had known only she would be paid $10 "upon publication," but she had expected some notification prior to a print date. She hadn't received any, but she couldn't have been happier with her discovery. She was now a published writer. Much later she described the exhilaration she felt, by saying, "The moment in which I saw that story in print was one of the happiest of my very happy life."

Maud Palmer Hart was born on April 26, 1892, to Thomas Walden Hart from Iowa and Stella Palmer Hart from Winnebago, a small town near Mankato. Her father had been in sales when he arrived in Mankato in 1883, and soon he was a partner in a wholesale-retail grocery store on Front Street. By the time Tom Hart opened his own shoe store, Kathleen and then Maud had joined the family; a third daughter, Helen, would follow shortly.

Maud's childhood was very happy. She played with her sisters and made friends easily. She was an extremely observant child who wanted to remember everything: every event, every landmark, and every person who crossed her path. Maud loved to read and spent many Saturday afternoons in the town's library. She also showed an early interest in local history.

Maud liked to write too. She started writing stories as soon as she could hold a pencil and often followed her mother around the house asking how to spell the words she wanted to use. Her childhood "writing room" was high in the backyard maple tree. Here she would compose stories, poems, and plays with titles like "The Repentance of Lady Clinton and Her Secret Marriage." Her father played an important role in encouraging her; his inspired suggestions were called "snoggestions" by the young girl. When she was ten, her father surprised her with a very special birthday present, one she would remember all her life. He collected some of her poems and had them bound into a booklet. This gift made Maud realize how much other people enjoyed her writings. She didn't want to disappoint them or herself, and she began to take her writing seriously.

Knowing so young that she wanted to be a writer was providential for Maud. She spent many hours assembling scrapbooks and writing in diaries while she was growing up. She knew that to write about what was near and dear to her, she would need to recall in detail all the sights and smells and feelings of her childhood. She filled notebook after notebook with stories. One of her favorite pastimes was to illustrate the stories with pictures cut from popular magazines.

Life was good for the Harts. Maud's father was elected treasurer of Blue Earth County. (Mankato sits where the Blue Earth River joins the Minnesota River.) The post was quite an honor, and Tom soon moved his family into a bigger house, just a block from the courthouse. Maud was sad to leave the comfortable neighborhood that had held so many memories and such dear friends. She would forever remember climbing the sprawling maple tree to do her writing, and she would also miss her baths in the kitchen and the old coal stove and burning embers by which she had read her precious books. But Maud was set to enter high school and so, looking toward the future, she accepted the change. In the new house there was a music room where Kathleen could practice her singing; she would become a professional opera singer in Minneapolis. Each sister had her own bedroom and bathroom, so privacy would no longer be a problem. Maud's new house was close to school, and soon her home became the "hangout" for classmates.

After high school graduation in 1910, Maud faced another move. She enrolled at the University of Minnesota in Minneapolis, but things did not go well for her there. She was trying to attend classes, study, and get good grades while recovering from an appendix operation. When she arrived home for the Thanksgiving holidays, her family saw she was not well. They encouraged her take a trip west to visit her grandmother.

And that's how it happened that it was in California that Maud sold her first story; she was just eighteen years old. She returned to the University of Minnesota the next semester and took classes that would help with her writing. She began working for the *Minnesota Daily* newspaper and *Minnesota Magazine*. It wasn't long before she met a young man, Russell McCord, to whom she became engaged—several times. But something was just not right, and she kept breaking the engagement.

Maud became women's editor of the *Minnesota Daily*, and she continued her writing: "Her Story" was published in *Minnesota Magazine* in 1912. One of the turning points in her career was a letter of praise from the famous professor Dr. Maria Sanford. Sanford had joined the University of Minnesota in 1880, when the school boasted a student body of 300. She had been the first woman professor at the college and eventually became head of the English Department. Sanford was well known for the concern she had for all of her students. She spent long hours poring over student essays and coaching oratory teams. She was loved by her students, who appreciated her use of lantern slides to bring life to daily lessons. There was no campus housing and students often had to travel great distances to attend classes, so Sanford bought a large home near the university and offered housing to sixteen students. She gave parties and socials in her home so students could get to know each other and interact with their peers. Her reputation and her innovative teaching methods put her in demand as a guest lecturer across the state. She was officially praised by the superintendent of schools for her hard work. As an ambassador of learning, Sanford was named "Best Loved Woman in Minnesota." Though it might not have been what Sanford hoped for, Maud, after receiving Sanford's letter applauding her work and encouraging her to keep writing, left college for good.

Her next adventure was a trip to Europe, sailing from Boston on the *Canopie* in 1914. Maud spent a great deal of time in Paris and collected rich writing material that she would later use. While there she met a young architect, Paulo Conte, who fell madly in love with her. The young Frenchman proposed marriage, but Maud was not tempted by his offer; she returned home to Minnesota alone. But love was on the horizon for the attractive dark-haired young woman.

In the spring of 1917, Maud was hired by the Wakefield Publicity Bureau. It was through Mrs. Wakefield's matchmaking that Maud met Delos Wheeler Lovelace, a journalist and writer. Maud was intrigued by the young man even before she met him. She had read some of his writings and she loved the images evoked by his last name, Lovelace. She was happy that he was from Minnesota, knowing that they would have many interests to share. Delos was from Brainerd, a resort lake town north of Minneapolis on the Mississippi River. By the time Delos met Maud, he was a seasoned journalist, having worked on the *Fargo Courier, Minnesota Daily News,* and the *Minneapolis Tribune.* This time twenty-five-year-old Maud had no doubts about accepting a proposal of marriage. The couple was wed in the Hart home eight months later on Thanksgiving Day, November 29, 1917.

In 1918, the summer after the Lovelaces were married, Delos was sent to the war zone in Europe. He returned safely in 1919, and soon after the couple moved to New York City where Delos began work as a reporter on the *Daily News.* Maud submerged herself in researching a book idea she had, one based on her Uncle Frank's renegade life.

Maud and Delos were blessed with their first child on February 12, 1925. But tragedy struck the blissfully happy parents. The infant boy lived only three hours. To escape the constant daily reminders of their tragedy, Maud and Delos moved back to the Minnesota life they loved. They purchased a small home at Casco Point, a secluded spot on Lake Minnetonka just west of Minneapolis. Here the couple enjoyed the fresh, clean air filled with loon calls echoing across the lake. Maud wrote some short stories that were published in *Ainslee's* and *Sunset.* Delos wrote stories too; they were published in *The Saturday Evening Post* and *Ladies' Home Journal.*

Maud was still trying to develop the story she had been researching back in New York. Delos encouraged her to turn her ideas into a novel, and so, incorporating her love of history, Maud began to write a historical novel set in Minnesota. Alex, the main character of the book, would be based on her errant Uncle Frank, who had defied his stepfather and run away from home at the age of seventeen to join a traveling opera troupe. The hushed stories of his adventurous exploits and his eventual marriage to an older actress that she had heard as a child found fertile ground in Maud's imagination. Her first book, *The Black Angels,* was published in 1926. The "Angels" of the title were the members of the Andrews Opera Company, with whom Frank had sung. The *New York Times* gave Maud's novel a favorable review and called it "genuinely pleasing."

Maud was excited by the success of her first novel and immediately began a second one. Her next novel would be a historical romance set in Fort Snelling, Minnesota, around 1830. To get the detailed facts she needed to make her book historically accurate, Maud and Delos moved into a Saint Paul hotel for the winter of 1926–27. It was close to the Minnesota Historical Society, where she would do most of her archival work. Then the couple moved back to the lake in the spring, and Maud began writing her story of Delia DuGay and Jasper Page.

In 1928 Maud and Delos returned to New York City. Delos would be writing for the *New York Sun,* and she would finish her second novel, *Early Candlelight.* The book was published in 1929 and was a huge success. The *New York Times* review read: "Like a fresh wind sweeping in from her own breezy prairie comes this romance of early Minnesota, delightfully told by one of her native daughters." (*Early Candlelight* was reissued in 1949 by the University of Minnesota Press for the Minnesota Territory Centennial celebration in recognition of the book's historical accuracy. It was reprinted again in 1992 to celebrate the one-hundredth anniversary of Maud's birth.) Next Maud wrote *The Tune Is in the Tree,* and in 1930 Maud and Delos cowrote *Gentleman from England.*

Though their lives were very busy, the couple was delighted when Maud became pregnant. Little did they know that the upcoming birth of their only child would open an important new chapter in Maud's writing career. A daughter whom they named Merian was born on January 18, 1931, in New York City. Maud loved being a mother. She especially liked reading books to her young daughter. However, her happy life was also marked with sadness. In 1936 her dear father passed away. Maud's mother came to live with her until her death in 1947.

Merian grew strong and healthy, and her passion to hear and rehear the stories that her mother told of her Mankato childhood stirred up deep feelings in Maud. By 1938 Maud decided to put some of Merian's favorite stories down on paper; then she entered the manuscript in a contest sponsored by the Thomas Y. Crowell Company. When editor Elizabeth Riley read the submission, she knew it was something unique. Riley became Maud's friend and acted as her editor and publisher throughout the 1940s and 1950s. And so *Betsy-Tacy*, the first in a series of ten children's books, was born in 1940. It was set in 1897 when Betsy Ray was almost five. Maud had intended to write only one book, but the success of her novel was immediate and readers clamored for more. The rest of the series followed in a steady pattern until the last, *Betsy's Wedding*. Published in 1955, it was set in 1914 and followed Betsy as she graduated from high school, traveled through Europe, and walked down the aisle to marry the love of her life.

Maud used all the details that she had saved in notebooks and diaries to create memorable reading experiences for her young readers. The title character, Betsy (Elizabeth Warrington), who sports two brown braids and wants to be a writer, was based on herself, and she gave her hometown of Mankato the new name of "Deep Valley." Her sister Kathleen became Julia, a dramatic girl who becomes a professional singer, and her younger sister Helen debuted as Margaret, a studious child who wears hair ribbons. Maud loved bringing all her childhood places and people to life. Betsy's friend Tacy Kelly has a strong sense of fun just like Frances "Bick" Kenny, Maud's dearest friend. Tib, another character, came from Marjorie "Midge" Gerlach, a petite golden-haired friend.

Her childhood was "the happiest childhood a child could possibly know," Maud had said many times, and she filled her books with sleigh rides, socials, and friendship. But she also included some of the bad times: a baby dies; Tacy gets very ill with diphtheria. The books closely mirrored Maud's life, and her own child, Merian, helped her to remember the feelings and character-istic nuances of each age. By the time she was writing about Betsy's graduation, her own daughter was graduating, and when Merian went off to Smith College, Maud was writing *Carney's House Party*. During the writing of *Betsy's Wedding*, Merian was married to Engle-bert Kirchner, a magazine editor

The Lovelaces moved to Claremont, California, a college town, in 1953. Maud's sisters had relocated out west and Maud still had a deep affection for sunny California, where she had sold her first story. Maud worked on her last book, *The Valentine Box* and worked with Delos to help found Claremont's first Episcopal Church, Saint Ambrose. Maud's beloved husband and helper died of a heart attack in January 1967, just before their fiftieth wedding anniversary. Maud continued to write of her Mankato home. She authored more than twenty-five books, and all reflect her deep-set Midwestern ideals of friendship and family.

The Betsy-Tacy children's series took on a life of its own. The books have been popular since the day the first book was pub-lished. Even though they are set at the turn of the twentieth cen-tury, they espouse a modern theme. The young girls in the books aspire to be writers and performers and professional women, and they succeed. The books were included in the 1974 feminist pub-lication, "Miss Muffet Fights Back," a list of recommended books in which girls are portrayed in positive roles. The Mankato Branch of the American Association of University Women sponsored a Betsy-Tacy Days celebration, and the mayor of Mankato pro-claimed October 7, 1961, Betsy-Tacy Day. Maud lived well beyond the Betsy-Tacy Day proclamation and was always astounded at the many accolades she received.

Maud Hart Lovelace died on March 11, 1980. Her ashes are interred in Glenwood cemetery in Mankato, but her legacy lives on. The Betsy-Tacy Society, a national organization based in Mankato and more than a 1,000 members strong, promotes the continued reading of her books. In 1997 a national three-day convention was held in her hometown to celebrate the one-hundredth anniversary of Betsy's five-year-old birthday party, when she and Tacy first became friends. Several hundred devotees attended.

Each year since 1980, the year of Maud's death, a Minnesota reading contest established in her honor attracts hundreds of students. The winner is announced on her birthday, April 25. The children's wing of the Minnesota Valley Regional Library in Mankato was named for her, and Mankato artist Marian Anderson painted a mural of Maud, her friends, and various local sites depicted in her books. Children today can enjoy a character re-enactment of Maud Hart Lovelace in the *Families* exhibit of the History Center Museum Theater, and fans can take a Betsy-Tacy walking tour of Mankato. In the 1998 movie *You've Got Mail*, Meg Ryan's character, a bookstore owner, recommends Betsy-Tacy books to her customer. Today the Betsy-Tacy series ranks as one of the best-selling children's fiction of all time.

Maud Hart Lovelace's spirit lives on in the hundreds of children who read her books. They are often amazed that Maud really did "live in a little yellow house at the end of a street which stopped at the bottom of a big hill." Maud was surprised by her fame. Her words reflect her happy life, "I am, nevertheless, glad that I chose writing and, if I had to do it all over, I would choose the same way."

Marjorie Child Husted

1892–1986

Boardroom Pioneer

*M*arjorie set out for the Nicollet Hotel and was soon caught up in the downtown rush. She flew down Hennepin Avenue and strolled through the lush park grounds of Gateway Center. Then she passed through the doors of the grand Nicollet Hotel. The lobby was lavish in its plush carpeting and dark wood-paneled walls. Designed in 1923 by Holabird and Roche in a Colonial Revival style, the hotel was one of the stately landmarks of the city. But she could not stop to appreciate the fine architectural details. Marjorie was headed to the top floor, which housed the radio studios of WCCO. She was excited thinking about the thousands of women waiting to hear her latest home-making advice. Marjorie loved her job, and this new radio program would be a milestone in her already extraordinary career. She had been the driving force behind the Gold Medal Flour symbol for years, but now she would also be the voice. It was March 4, 1925, and Marjorie was a major cog in the wheel that would immortalize the endurable American icon that came to be known as Betty Crocker. She was ready to begin the *Betty Crocker*

Cooking School of the Air broadcast. Marjorie walked boldly to the microphone, cleared her throat, and began.

Marjorie was born in 1892 in Minneapolis, Minnesota, to Sampson Reed Child, a lawyer, and Alice Alberta Webber, a homemaker, and she was one of four children, two girls and two boys. The Childs were a proud American family tracing their heritage back to the founding of America in the 1600s. Marjorie grew up like most children who lived in the bustling city. She attended public grade school and then went on to West High School. Marjorie was an active student who showed early signs of an insatiable drive for achievement. She was a member of the school's social club, and she participated in drama and athletics. Despite her numerous extracurricular activities, Marjorie was a Latin scholar and a member of the Kappa Alpha Theta honor society. An entry in her yearbook characterized her as having "a tender heart; a will inflexible."

Her first venture into the business world was selling animal incubators at the state fair. Her father had acquired a stall of wares from a client in lieu of cash, and Marjorie, offering the equipment to attending farmers, tasted business success for the first time. She would remember years later that a fortune-teller at the fair told her she would make money through her own efforts one day, but Marjorie thought the idea was crazy. How could a woman make enough money on her own to get by? But times were changing; the country was experiencing a growth in manufacturing due to the increased use of mass production techniques. The industrial revolution meant more employment opportunities for women.

Marjorie was intent on excelling in her college studies at the University of Minnesota. She earned a bachelor of arts in German at graduation in 1913 and a bachelor of education in home economics the year after that. She felt ready to officially enter the business world at last.

Marjorie Child Husted

CORBIS/BETTMANN ©1950

Her first job was as a secretary with the Infant Welfare Society of Minneapolis. Soon World War I was raging in Europe, and Marjorie began working for the Red Cross in the information and publicity bureau of the home office in the northern division. A very capable worker, she was later promoted to assistant director of the field service.

After the war Marjorie became the director of the bureau of information of the Woman's Cooperative Alliance, an organization that worked with parents' groups to prevent juvenile delinquency. But she was still concerned with finding her niche, a job that would bring her the money to support herself, as the carnival gypsy had foretold.

Her next job, in 1923, with the Creamette Company of Minneapolis doing promotional advertising and merchandising, was the one that would change her career path and her future. She was finally using her home economics degree, and she felt she had come a long way when, just a year later, she was hired as the home economics field representative by the Washburn-Crosby Company.

This Minneapolis-based mill enterprise was the parent company of Gold Medal Flour. Cadwallader C. Washburn had built his flour mill on the banks of the Mississippi River where it ran through the fledging town of Minneapolis. He had bought out a failing mill and spent $100,000 to construct a new, modern operation. Locals believed this was a foolish idea and called the six-story structure that graced Saint Anthony Falls, "Washburn's Folly." Washburn's mill was the largest in the area, putting out nearly 840 barrels of flour a day. Many said the large mill could not survive so far west, but it was milling entrepreneurs with a vision like Washburn who contributed to the early growth of the state. The flour mill eventually became the Washburn-Crosby Company as new partners and a new automated mill were added to the business. Its 5,500 barrels a day was without significant competition until a man named Pillsbury starting his company in 1881. The Washburn-Crosby Company reached the pinnacle of success when in 1880 it exhibited its remarkably fine flour at the first Miller's International Exhibition in Cincinnati and was awarded the top three prizes. It won the bronze medal for its "Parisian" flour, the silver medal for "Extra" flour, and, in what would go down in history as one of the longest-lived product names of the twentieth century, the gold medal for "Superlative" flour. Less than two months later, "Gold Medal" became the brand name for Washburn-Crosby's best grade of flour and appeared on all sacks headed out the door.

Just two years before Marjorie went to work at Crosby-Washburn, the company had stumbled over another successful business maneuver. In 1921 a Gold Medal advertisement had included a jigsaw puzzle that offered a prize to those who could successfully assemble and return it to the company. The completed puzzle showed a scene of people carrying Gold Medal flour sacks. Surprisingly there were more than 30,000 completed puzzles mailed in along with letters asking for recipes and answers to baking questions. The company knew it had discovered a new marketing tactic. Because the team hired to answer the avalanche of mail was all men, the first step was to come up with a name that would reflect a woman's persona. "Crocker" was selected in honor of a retired director of the company, and "Betty" was chosen because it had a friendly and wholesome sound. The women employees of the company participated in a contest to develop the standard "signature" to be used by "Betty Crocker."

The twentieth century had witnessed a rise in home economics as an educational discipline. Domestic science became an avenue that women could use to enter the corporate world. During this time women also realized that there was information available to help them run their daily lives, lives that had suddenly been altered by world events. World War I, the Great Depression, World War II, and the drive of young women to go to college and seek professional work outside the home all meant that doing things the old way, their mothers' way, was not working. Reacting to the growing need of American housewives to have more information about new ways of cooking, baking, and preparing meals, the company began to sponsor cooking schools across the country, hosted by trained home economists. Within a couple of years, the staff of women who directed the Home Service Department numbered twenty-one, and Marjorie was among the chosen few.

It was a demanding job that took Marjorie to cooking schools and meeting halls in small prairie towns across six states. She often lectured to standing-room-only crowds of women who wanted to learn the basics of cooking and bread-making. Marjorie was paying her dues, and soon opportunity was again knocking on her door.

In 1924 a campaign involving a series of daytime radio shows was launched at WLAG radio in Minneapolis. Marjorie introduced *Betty Crocker's Cooking School of the Air*, the first woman's food service program to go national. Marjorie provided Betty's voice, and her advice was broadcast across the country. The format of the program included cooking tips, music, information on new products, recipes, "kitchen-tested" menus, and dramatizations of listeners' letters. An early theme was "Interviews with Eligible Bachelors," who discussed their domestic expectations when looking for a bride. Betty Crocker herself received hundreds of marriage proposals.

On October 2, 1924, the booming flour company bought WLAG, the "Call of the North" radio station located in the Minneapolis Oak Grove Hotel. The station had been struggling since it took to the air waves on September 4, 1922. Its call letters were changed to WCCO to represent the Washburn-Crosby Company, and the studio was moved to the twelfth and thirteen floors of the Nicollet Hotel. With its twin aerial transmitter towers, it was the largest radio station west of the Mississippi. After only one year, the *Betty Crocker Cooking School of the Air* was picked up by thirteen regional stations. Marjorie was delighted. Graduates of the program's cooking school numbered 238 the first year. It was at WCCO's studios that Marjorie met her future husband, broadcaster K. Wallace Husted. She often described him with his dashing good looks as a Clark Gable look-alike. After a short engagement they were married in October 1925. Marjorie continued with her Betty Crocker activities running a home service department for Washburn-Crosby, and answering letters from consumers on topics of homemaking.

On June 24, 1928, several mills in the area combined operations and formed a new corporation, General Mills. Washburn-Crosby gave the new organization both the Gold Medal Flour label and its Betty Crocker name and home service department. The department was renamed the Betty Crocker Homemaking Service in 1929, and Marjorie was chosen as its director. General Mills would become the world's largest flour mill and cereal producer.

Marjorie was still running the radio program, but her role as the Betty Crocker spokesperson was expanding. She made public appearances and lectured to housewives across the nation, disseminating Betty Crocker's advice on a vast range of homemaking topics. She traveled to Hollywood to interview celebrities for her radio show. She met many famous people including movie stars Joan Crawford, Jean Harlow, Helen Hayes, and Clark Gable. She encouraged Hollywood stars to talk about their personal lives, and when Margaret Sullavan and Jean Harlow, known for their model-like figures, admitted they loved to eat bread, General Mills was ecstatic. Washburn-Crosby had been publishing cookbooks under the Gold Medal name since 1880 and continued, now using the Betty Crocker name. Part of Marjorie's Hollywood assignment was to get recipes and testimonials from famous people to put into these cookbooks. The 1933 cookbook contained entries by movie actresses Mary Pickford and Claudette Colbert. The cookbook sold for 25 cents.

The Great Depression years hit American families hard. Women struggled to stretch tight budgets. Many housewives wanted to know what foods could be bought economically. Marjorie was not just a voice on the radio or a hand behind the famous signature; she was also Betty's essence, advising homemakers on how to use their food money wisely. Marjorie felt for the women who wrote in not just for recipes but to share their lives. They talked about their children and their husbands, and they often included stories of love and hope. Marjorie put sincerity behind every piece of advice she gave to homemakers. She spoke in a warm tone that inspired women, nurturing and shaping the spirit of the American homemaker.

The *Betty Crocker Cooking School of the Air* program would eventually go national as part of the National Broadcasting Company (NBC) and run for twenty-four years without interruption, reaching more than one million listeners every day. Many of these would register for the Betty Crocker Cooking School. The radio station, WCCO, would be bought by the Columbia Broadcasting System and added to its lineup of outstanding stations. It would move from the Nicollet Hotel to the Elks Club, which had a large auditorium for program production.

Marjorie felt she owed something to the world that had accepted her as a businesswoman, and she often mentored younger women. She was remembered fondly by Nielsine Hansen Gehrke, who was a young journalist on the *Virginia Daily Enterprise* when she met Marjorie. The *Daily Enterprise* was a small paper in northern Minnesota, and although Nielsine wanted to branch out and tackle a big city market, she had many reservations. Marjorie encouraged

Nielsine in her work and inspired her to take the chance when a Chicago offer came her way. Later, when a position opened up at General Mills, Nielsine was invited by Marjorie to come to Minneapolis and become a Betty Crocker assistant. The young woman accepted and was soon conducting cooking schools across the country. She was astounded that at one session more than 1,000 people were in attendance.

Until 1936 Betty Crocker was a voice without a face. As it became more and more evident that consumers wanted to identify with an actual person, Marjorie knew she had to put a face to the growing corporate identity. Consumers hungered for Betty Crocker and her sage advice as much as they were hungry for the products she recommended. It was time for Betty Crocker's first formal portrait. She called in Neysa McMein, an outstanding New York illustrator, and commissioned her to do a portrait of the already legendary character. McMein was delighted to do the artwork. She had been providing covers for *McCall's* and had created advertising graphics for Palmolive and Lucky Strike ad campaigns. She jumped to the task of bringing life to the woman whose name was on every homemaker's lips. Ironically, the brown-haired, blue-eyed, advice-giving symbol of domestication resembled Marjorie herself, and soon McMein's womanly image of the fictional Betty Crocker began to appear on consumer packages and in company ads.

(Betty Crocker's face has been updated eight times since McMein's original portrait. Her most recent portrait was done in 1996 and resulted from a computer simulation of all her previous portraits, plus the morphing of seventy-five images submitted by consumers who were asked to create their "ideal" Betty Crocker. She now wears a suit instead of a housedress and has changed from a matriarchal figure to a younger, modern-looking woman.)

Meanwhile business was booming at General Mills and so were the cooking schools, where a staff of well-trained professionals tested and demonstrated products and recipes. In 1944 more than 70,000 housewives were enrolled in the Betty Crocker Home Legion—a program that Marjorie had created. She felt a woman's role as a homemaker had been underrecognized, and she wanted to encourage young women to view homemaking as a worthy career.

By 1945 *Fortune* magazine called Betty Crocker "the woman best known to housewives of the U.S." and described Marjorie's department as "a blend of woman's club, tearoom, cooking school, and business office." The staff of nutritionists, cooks, advertising professionals, and home economists all worked well under Marjorie's supervision. By 1949 her staff numbered forty people.

During World War II Marjorie used the Betty Crocker radio program to advise homemakers on scarce foods and won awards for suggesting ways to deal with product shortages. She felt strongly about women's issues and in the "Design for Happiness" segment of her show, women discussed for the first time on the public airwaves the intense feelings they had about being alone, overburdened, and underappreciated. Marjorie could relate to these women because at this time she was also alone. Her husband was serving in the Red Cross in Europe.

In 1948 Marjorie's hard work paid off again. She became a General Mills consultant in advertising, public relations, and home service. This was a position equivalent to vice president and, for a woman of the late 1940s, truly an accomplishment in the male-dominated world of business. She also proudly served as consultant to the United States Department of Agriculture in its nationwide food conservation program. Marjorie had worked long and hard to build her career, and she enjoyed the recognition. She felt she had greatly contributed to the Betty Crocker success when in February of 1948 a *Business Week* survey reported that 91 percent of homemakers recognized the name Betty Crocker. As a result of her accomplishments, Marjorie was named Advertising Woman of the

Year in 1948 by the Advertising Federation of America, the first home economist to win the award.

But there was a greater honor in store for her, and for this she would have to travel to Washington, D.C. She was extremely proud to be recognized as Woman of the Year by the Women's National Press Club for her outstanding achievement in business. She was the first businesswoman ever to be so recognized and she took the stage on May 14, 1949, with Eleanor Roosevelt and Anna Mary "Grandma" Moses to receive the special plaque presented by the guest of honor, President Harry S. Truman.

It was hard to come down from the euphoria of such success, but there was still much to be done. Marjorie got to work helping to research and edit the *Betty Crocker Picture Cookbook*. Published in 1950, the book of recipes, cooking tips, and color photos was an immediate success, and today, after numerous reprintings, has sold more than forty-five million copies.

Marjorie worked very hard, but she never forgot that there was important work to do outside of the General Mills office. Her work in the community kept her very busy. Marjorie was president of the Minnesota Home Economics Association in 1949 and served as the chair of the Public Relations Council of the American Home Economics Association. She was a member of the Nutrition Council of the American Red Cross, the Home Economics Committee of the Cereal Institute, and the Women's Advertising Club of Minneapolis. She also put her energies into activities of the Minneapolis Unitarian Church and her hobbies of tennis and hiking. She belonged to the Minneapolis Historical Society, the Symphony Orchestra and the Young Women's Christian Association.

Eventually Marjorie felt the time was right to leave General Mills and get off the corporate ladder. She had come to feel that the corporation was not doing enough to recognize women and their fight for equal rights, and she often spoke in her lectures of how the letters from desperate women made her sad. She had not been looked on favorably when, as a newly promoted consultant, she had moved her secretary, of course a female, into the executive offices along with her. Her article for the *Journal of Home Economics*, "Would You Like More Recognition?" spoke about empowering women; it was probably a hard pill to swallow for her male co-workers. Certainly her "bias quiz"—a short quiz she developed to show men (even those who thought they were unbiased) that they were indeed close-minded when it came to women and their abilities and position in the workplace—was not accepted well.

Marjorie took a different path and formed her own consulting firm, Marjorie Child Husted and Associates, in April 1950. From here she could champion women's rights without fear of reprisal. She joined the National Committee on the Status of Women and was active in the American Association of University Women and the National Committee on the Status of Women. In a 1978 interview she called herself a "feminist."

The brown-haired, blue-eyed, 5'7" woman on whom the first Betty Crocker likeness was fashioned died in Minneapolis, Minnesota, on December 23, 1986, at age 94.

Today Betty Crocker gets up to 100,000 calls and letters from consumers every year. But perhaps Marjorie's best claim to fame comes in her support of a woman's place in the workforce. She was very conscious of how hard it was for a woman to succeed in a large corporation. She hated the double standard that women were held to, and she often tried to circumvent the establishment in order to help other women. In a 1939 letter she discussed how she wanted to keep Marguerite, one of her workers, even though she would have to go against company policy. "I have run into the problem, however, that the Company has now set a very definite rule not to employ married women." She then went on to say that she would also have to hide the fact that Marguerite had a child because this would give management even more reason not to hire her.

Marjorie's advice to homemakers was practical yet clever, and above all she reassured women that they could indeed handle their responsibilities as wives and mothers while pursuing other interests. The longevity of the Betty Crocker icon is a credit to a task well done and a testimony to her impact on American women. The milling complex she called home for so long is now a National Historic Landmark. The intelligent and capable woman who balanced career and family was honored when the Twin Cities celebrated Marjorie Child Husted Day. Her groundbreaking work for women in the workplace lives on today.

WANDA GAG
1893–1946

Innovative Children's Book
Illustrator and Writer

*E*rnestine Evans felt the promise of something special blowing in the wind that day in 1926 as she slipped away from her job as children's book editor at the publishing house of Coward-McCann to enjoy a little free time. She had heard of a wonderful art show at New York's Weyhe Gallery featuring the works of Wanda Gag, an exciting new artist from Minnesota. Ernestine strolled through the gallery and liked what she saw. The pictures were new and unique. Ernestine spied the artist, a slim young woman with curling brown hair. Her eyes were intense, with an artist's passion. Ernestine boldly strode up to the dark beauty and presented her with a challenge. She asked Wanda to write and illustrate a children's story for her publishing company to consider.

Wanda was more than ready to tackle the assignment. She went home that evening and, reaching into her past, dusted off "Millions of Cats," a story she had written years ago to amuse her friends' children. It had been soundly rejected by more than one publisher! Wanda wondered what Ernestine would make of it.

MINNESOTA HISTORICAL SOCIETY

Wanda Gag

"Millions of Cats" was the story of a lonely old couple's search for a feline companion. Wanda had meticulously hand-lettered the text and had integrated her illustrations in the copy. Ernestine was delighted with Wanda's book, and *Millions of Cats* was published in 1928. A children's classic was born.

Wanda Hazel Gag was born on March 11, 1893, to Anton and Elisabeth (Lissie) Biebl Gag in New Ulm, Minnesota. She was the first of seven children. Her parents, like many of New Ulm's Germans, encouraged the arts, drawing, dancing, and music in their home. Her Bohemian father was an artist, photographer, and painter who decorated houses and churches around the quaint town. He taught all of his children to paint and draw, duties that were as important as chores in the Gag household. Their family home was decorated with original hand paintings and drawings on the walls. Wanda grew up in this mixed artistic culture and was to write later in *The Junior Book of Authors*, "This neat little German town gave me a background so European that I often forget that I have never been outside of America." Old-World customs, Bavarian and Bohemian folk songs, music and endless hours of storytelling by family members could not help but influence Wanda's artistic style and subject matter. Speaking only German in her home, Wanda did not learn English until she was sent off to school. Though money was tight, the Gags always seemed to enjoy a spirited and eventful life, one that incubated the artistic dreams of a young girl.

Childhood in New Ulm was fun and challenging for Wanda. The small town was situated on high ground that was once an island in the glacial River Warren. Founded in 1854 by the German Land Association of Minnesota, it was named after the cathedral city of Ulm in Wurttemberg, Germany. The lush area of the town consisted of three levels of terraces lining the confluence of the Minnesota and Cottonwood Rivers. The residential section was the highest of the terraces, and this was where the Gags raised their brood of artistic children. Their home, built in 1894, was a large two-story house on North Washington Street, with a second-story porch above the entrance to the front door. The next terrace down was the business district, then at the lowest level stood the railroad station. Wanda loved the neat and tidy town where German was spoken on the streets and was proud of the Hermann Monument, a 102-foot statue of a German chief who had defeated Roman conquerors in A.D. 9. The statue was a landmark of the city. New Ulm's architect and builder Julius Berndt first came up with the idea modeled on a similar statue that had been erected in Germany.

The cornerstone for the project was set in 1888, before Wanda was born, but the Center Street monument was not ready for dedication until 1897. By then Wanda was four years old. The photographs her father took of the huge statue covered with scaffolding, standing high on a bluff overlooking the river's broad valley in Hermann Monument Park and the city of New Ulm, were part of her family's history. The base of the huge monument, made of Minnesota limestone, supported the statue and the beautiful and expansive dome above it. The dome atop the monument could be reached by climbing a winding staircase, and here visitors could look out the windows at all the angles of their lovely city. The cultural life of New Ulm was fertile and enriched Wanda's artistic temperament. Wanda and her childhood friend, Olga Mayer, spent long hours writing stories together, completing about twenty-two of them.

When Wanda was fourteen, the unthinkable happened and her life was changed forever. Wanda's father was dying of tuberculosis, and although Minnesota's well-touted environs had brought thousands of invalids to the area to be cured, there was no cure for her father. He died in 1908, leaving his family virtually destitute.

On his deathbed her father had whispered to Wanda that he wanted her to pursue her art and become the great artist he had not. Wanda was only fourteen and she wanted to obey her beloved father's dying request, but she also recognized how sickly her mother had become caring for her dying father. She understood that before she could follow her artistic ambitions, she would first have to become the main provider for her family of six sisters and a brother, the youngest of whom was only one year old. Immediately Wanda began writing and illustrating stories for the *Minneapolis Junior Journal*, a Sunday supplement section of the *Minneapolis Journal*, a newspaper aimed at the youth market. Constantly honing her writing and artistic skills, she took on any art-related work she could that would bring in much-needed money. The family wore used clothing given to them by local charities and tried to stretch their food budget beyond realistic boundaries.

Fortunately they were able to keep the house, but doing so meant that housework, wood chopping, and screaming children became part of Wanda's daily routine. It was an arduous time, but Wanda was determined to keep her family together despite benevolent offers to adopt some of the younger children. If she wanted to keep her family intact, some people said she should put aside her art. Friends suggested she get a more secure job, but Wanda persisted; she knew she could make a living using her artistic talent. She had high expectations of herself and of everyone else in her family and set high school graduation for herself and all her siblings as their goal. This meant a profound commitment on her part and a great need for money. The family was barely getting by and Wanda was working all the hours she could.

In 1910 Wanda won a statewide art contest sponsored by the St. Paul Institute of Arts and the *Brown County Journal*, Wanda's local newspaper. She was only a junior in high school, but her drawing of a young girl seated at a table announced to the world that Wanda's talent was in drawing common, everyday things. She would find subject matter in the landscape and home life that was part of her personal world. The second-place medal she won was accolade enough to feed her artistic wellspring at a time when things were very difficult for her.

In 1912 Wanda somehow managed to finish high school with distinction, winning awards for her art as well as an art scholarship at the prestigious St. Paul Institute of Arts. The scholarship was not enough to meet all her expenses, and Wanda would have to raise some money before she could begin her studies. She obtained her teaching certificate during the summer after graduation and then took a position as a teacher in Springfield, Minnesota, for a year to raise some funds to support her family while she attended art school in the Twin Cities. She took in work on the side, painting lamp shades, illustrating magazine covers, and designing calendars. When two of her younger sisters finished high school the next year and found jobs as teachers, Wanda felt comfortable enough to leave them in charge and head to Saint Paul to take advantage of the scholarship she had won the year before.

Wanda attended the St. Paul Institute from 1913 to 1914 and the prestigious Minneapolis School of Art from 1914 to 1917. It was during this time that she illustrated her first book, *A Child's Book of Folk-Lore, Mechanics of Written English: A Drill in the Use of Caps and Points through the Rimes of Mother Goose.* She had become interested in a unique art form of letter illustration and would try her hand at it again soon.

But misfortune was to strike the Gag family once more. Wanda's mother died in 1917, and Wanda again faced the loss of a loved one close to her heart. She was very sad and yet knew she had to keep moving on. She had no choice but to bring the younger children to live with her in Minneapolis while she finished her last year of art school. It was not an easy time, but with the support of family and friends, her hard work paid off. Not only did she graduate, but she also won a much-coveted art scholarship to the famous Art Students League in New York City for the school year 1917–18. She was one of only fifteen recipients of the national awards.

Attending school in New York City where things were not cheap while still trying to attend to the needs of her family back in New Ulm, Wanda again had to take on odd jobs so she could earn extra money to send home. She found work as a commercial artist and fashion designer, but this kind of work was not her passion and she longed to turn away from the commercial scene. Years later Wanda wrote in *The Junior Book of Authors*: "I did not care for that future. The strain of expressing other people's ideas, when my own were clamoring for attention, became too great." She was living with a family in New York and managed to find some time to write and illustrate children books—including her book eventually published as *Millions of Cats*—to amuse the children in the family. Although she could not get them published at the time, the exercise provided a good creative outlet for her. She struggled along for years torn between two worlds, one of passion and one of necessity. Then she made a decision.

It was time for a change. Wanda bought a small house in the Connecticut countryside and began to develop her artistic style. Her work was often fanciful, reminiscent of her Bohemian heritage, but she also felt deeply for the plight of the common person. She had lived in poverty and knew the value of hard work. Her art reflected her interest in working class men and women, and she often found her work among that of famous artists such as Cornelia Barns, Fred Ellis, William Gropper, and J. J. Lankes. One of her famous social commentary illustrations was used for the cover of the October 1924 issue of *The Liberator*, a monthly that aligned itself politically with the country's growing labor movement.

Her drawings eventually caught the attention of the Weyhe

Gallery in New York, and she soon had plans for her first one-woman show in 1926. The show, displaying her drawings, lithographs, and watercolors, was very successful, and the sales enabled Wanda to continue her artistic endeavors. It was here that Ernestine Evans from the Coward-McCann Publishing Company discovered Wanda Gag, the children's book author and illustrator.

Millions of Cats was an instant success. It was popular with young readers and won many awards, most notable the Newbery Honor Book Award. It won critical acclaim for its double-page illustrations and hand-lettered text—both revolutionary for picture books of the day. Wanda was quite happy with her latest accomplishment and felt she had at last found her artistic voice. *Millions of Cats* was soon followed by another picture book in 1929, *The Funny Thing*, also was recognized for Wanda's unique talents. She had finally found a way to combine her love of lithography, woodcutting, and drawing with her passion for writing.

By 1930, despite the woes of the Great Depression, Wanda had achieved a success she had never dreamed possible. Her children's books were in demand. Part of the realization that she was becoming a prominent artist was the knowledge that she had finally fulfilled her dying father's request. Wanda missed her family desperately and eventually was able to move all of her siblings to New York. She married her longtime friend Earle Marshall Humphreys and settled down in a one-hundred-year-old New Jersey farmhouse. Knowing her creativity was sure to flourish here, she named her home "All Creation." Her sister Flavia joined her and became a writer and illustrator in her own right, and her brother Howard also lived with her and illustrated some of Wanda's books.

She continued to work hard. *Snippy and Snappy* was the next children's picture book she produced, in 1931, and *ABC Bunny* was published in 1932. Art had become her life by now. Wanda could boast of her first prize at the Philadelphia Lithograph Show in

1930 and shows at the Weyhe Gallery in 1930 and 1940. She also had shows at the Museum of Modern Art in New York in 1939 and the Metropolitan Museum of Art in 1943. But none of these pleased her as much as having her children's stories published, and in 1942 she delighted her audiences with a new book, *Nothing At All*.

But she had much more work to do. In 1936 after she accepted a job to illustrate the story of Hansel and Gretel for the *New York-Herald Tribune*, Wanda began to recall her fascination with the stories she heard as a young child in her home in New Ulm. Hours of storytelling by her parents, aunts, uncles, even neighbors had not seemed unusual to Wanda and her siblings—it was part of daily life in New Ulm. She accepted as her next challenge the translation and illustration of sixteen original Grimm's Brothers fairy tales. It was a labor of love, and one of her books, *Snow White and the Seven Dwarfs*, was a stunning success. It received the Caldecott Honor Award in 1939.

When World War II flashed on the scene, Wanda was willing to do her part. She put aside some of her artistic drive and took a job with the Department of Defense and grew her own vegetables at All Creation. Just about this time, with husband Humphreys, Wanda produced a syndicated series of picture puzzles, *Wanda's Wonderland* and *St. Nicholas*, as well as a board game, *Pick-A-Path*. They also collaborated on *Happiwork Story Boxes*, cardboard boxes with scenes painted on the six sides for children to play with.

Wanda's contemporaries held her in great esteem, and she was c,onsidered important in the predominantly male world of modern art. An independent thinker, Gag readily engaged in the issues of the day. She wrote an article for *The Nation*, "These Modern Women: A Hotbed of Feminists," in 1927. She wrote that marriage and motherhood were not the only measures of a woman. In her later diaries she wrote frankly about sexuality and romantic relationships.

Wanda was diagnosed with lung cancer, and she died on June 27, 1946. Her body was cremated, and her ashes were strewn along the little path that led to her art studio at All Creation.

Wanda Gag has remained in the public eye largely due to her children's books. *Millions of Cats* has remained in print since it was published in 1928 and has been translated into Dutch, French, Japanese, and other languages. *Millions of Cats* has been made into a filmstrip, her story *The Fisherman and His Wife* has been made into a motion picture, and her translation of *Tales from Grimm* has been recorded on audiocassette.

Today the Brown County Historical Museum in New Ulm recalls the glory days of the artist and the turn-of-the-twentieth-century period. Wanda's childhood home still stands. It was bought by the Wanda Gag House Association and has been beautifully preserved and placed on the National Register of Historic Places. Restorative work and paint removal have uncovered some of the drawings that had decorated the walls of the Gag family home. Exquisite hand painting and original drawings have been restored to their former beauty. Wanda Gag would be pleased to know that her home will be used as a children's literature interpretive center. In 1993 New Ulm held a centennial celebration of Wanda Gag's birth with special events, a new biography of her life, and exhibits of her works. Darla Gebhard of the Brown County Historical Society said this of Wanda Gag: "Her art and literature always reflected on her early Minnesota childhood. She could take ordinary objects and make them beautiful."

JEANNETTE RIDLON PICCARD

1895–1981

Balloonist Extraordinaire

*J*eannette smiled as she accepted the bouquet of flowers from her three young sons John, Paul, and Donald. This would be a historic day, not only for the daring young woman and her family, but also for the entire world. A small American flag was raised in the cool, clear daybreak to celebrate the occasion, and strains of the "Star Spangled Banner" wafted out across the crowd. Forty thousand spectators were waiting, but Jeannette wanted to savor the moment just a little longer. She stood alone atop the gondola for a few more seconds, then joined the two passengers already inside, her husband, Jean, and the couple's pet turtle. The takeoff began at 6:51 A.M., and the inflated balloon slowly rose in the morning air, taking the pressurized passenger gondola aloft with it. They floated all morning rising higher and higher. After reaching an altitude of 57,579 feet, the hot air that propelled the balloon upward started to cool down, and the balloon began to descend. Jeannette felt vindicated at last. So many sponsors had dropped the project because they did not think a woman could pilot a hot air balloon and now she had done more than that. She had made history as the first woman to travel into the stratosphere

Jeannette R. Piccard

MINNESOTA HISTORICAL SOCIETY

(the altitude above the Earth's atmosphere in which a person cannot breathe without pressurization). When she stepped foot on solid ground, she was inundated by an eager press with requests for stories and interviews. She loved every minute of the excitement. She had fulfilled a daring dream and would become a symbol of courage for young women everywhere. When a reporter asked her if she would do it again, she replied, "Oh! Just give me the chance."

Jeannette was born in Chicago, Illinois, on January 5, 1895, to John and Emily Caroline (Robinson) Ridlon. Her uneventful childhood did not portend the ambitious and fearless woman she would become. Her father was an eminent orthopedic surgeon, and the large family could trace its genealogy back to the 1470s. Jeannette had three sisters and three brothers. But life was not all happiness for the Ridlons; an early tragedy struck the family when Beatrice, Jeannette's younger sister, died in infancy. Perhaps it was this early introduction to death that fostered a spiritual commitment in the young girl. She began to develop an interest in Christianity, and when she was eleven years old she decided she wanted to be an Episcopal priest. She knew women were not allowed to be priests, but she held the hope that it would be possible by the time she was ready to begin her religious studies. One evening she revealed this dream to her mother, and to her surprise, the reserved matriarch broke down crying and ran out of the room. Jeannette had never seen her proper Victorian mother run before and she knew that she hurt her deeply. Jeannette's interest in a religious life was never mentioned again in the Ridlon household. She had other modern ideas, and her father supported some of her early feminist views. Though most girls of the era did not seek a formal education, the well-respected physician encouraged his daughter to go to college.

Jeannette entered Bryn Mawr in 1914 and chose philosophy

as her major field in order to stay close to her religious passion. In 1916, while at Bryn Mawr, she wrote an essay, "Should Women Be Admitted to the Priesthood of the Anglican Church?"; perhaps it was an astute young woman's perceptive intuition of where her life would lead her nearly sixty years later. Jeannette earned her bachelor of arts degrees in philosophy and psychology in 1918, but her hope that women would be allowed to enter the General Theological Seminary in New York did not materialize. She changed her plans and opted for graduate school at the University of Chicago.

The adventure she had been seeking was about to begin. Turning away from philosophy and the humanities, she embarked on a scientific course and set as her goal a master's degree in organic chemistry. It was in this typically male-dominated discipline that she met the eccentric and brilliant professor Jean-Felix Piccard. He was an associate professor in chemistry, recently arrived from Switzerland. She was immediately taken with this impassioned chemist.

Piccard in turn respected the young woman's bright mind and daring spirit and their common interest in science led to a lifetime partnership. Jean had served in the Swiss Army lighter-than-air service and had flown balloons with his twin brother, Auguste, for scientific projects since 1913. Jeannette wanted to share the adventure and experimentation with Jean, and she wanted to be integrally involved in his work. The two were married in 1919, the same year Jeannette completed her master's degree.

The couple left for Switzerland and taught for a while in Lausanne. Here Jeannette was able to hear firsthand some of the stories of Jean and August's childhood as identical twins. A favorite story was the account of how Jean went into a barbershop and complained about how fast his beard grew. The barber assured him that he could shave him so close that he would stay clean-shaven for twenty-four hours or he would give him a free shave. Several hours later Auguste came in the barber's shop with a heavy day's growth and collected his free shave, leaving a perplexed barber behind.

A few years later the Piccards returned to the States to teach and carry on their work. Jean became a naturalized U.S. citizen. By 1933 the Piccard brothers had earned a solid reputation for their stratospheric experiments. They had found that surviving the stratosphere required an enclosed container that could withstand subzero temperatures and low pressure. When a balloonist died after going up 40,000 feet without a pressurized air container, the Piccards were in demand for their scientific knowledge.

When Jean was asked to work on the balloon and gondola for the 1933 World's Fair in Chicago, he jumped at the chance. He was continuing the work he and his brother had started in record-breaking balloon travel and exploration. He designed a pressurized, airtight cabin that could be lifted by a balloon inflated with hydrogen. The gondola was named the *Century of Progress* and its sponsors were expecting it to attain a record-breaking altitude. Jean was to command the flight and Tex Settle was to pilot it. At this time many countries were trying to set altitude records; Russia and Belgium seemed to be ahead. Men willing to risk their lives were featured in bold headlines every day; many of the stories ended with obituaries. Sponsors Goodyear-Zeppelin and Dow Chemical wanted a record for the United States. In the end, to decrease the weight load by half and assure a higher altitude, Jean gave up his spot on the flight. Jeannette was left to console her husband. He was very disappointed, but when the balloon suffered a gas valve problem upon liftoff and descended within fifteen minutes, failing in its mission, Jean knew his time had not yet come.

Out of the 1933 *Century of Progress* setback came success for the Piccards. Jean and Jeannette secured the rights to the gondola and balloon and began to refine and rebuild the used equipment.

Wanting their next flight to serve science, not glory, they were determined to control all aspects of the project. Jean would handle the experiments, but he needed a pilot for the mission. Jeannette did not have to be convinced; she was eager to get into the space race. She did not concern herself with the news of the three Russian fliers who had died trying to ascend into the stratosphere earlier in the year.

Jeannette looked around for a good flight instructor and found him in the person of famed 1927 Gordon Bennett Race prizewinner Ed Hill. She began her lessons on May 15, 1934, and totally enjoyed the experience. One day in early June on a balloon descent, Ed let some gas escape and reduced ballast, flying just over an orchard of apple trees. He reached out and plucked an apple blossom, smiling as he placed it behind his ear for Jeannette to admire. She soloed a month later on June 16. She had her license well before October 23, the date set for their stratospheric flight.

The Piccards were having trouble finding sponsors to fund their project. *National Geographic* had refused because Jeannette, a woman and a mother, wanted to be the pilot. They did not want the bad publicity should anything happen to her. Even Goodyear-Zeppelin and Dow Chemical, with whom Jean had worked on the *Century of Progress* flight, refused. Dow asked that its name be taken off the gondola and that its trade name "Dowmetal" not be used. The Piccards eventually raised funds through private backers, and Henry Ford offered his facilities at Ford Airport for a launch site.

The takeoff went well. Jean blew open the external ballast bags and began the ascent. There was a slight problem with one of the drift rings, but the balloon rose steadily, reaching an altitude of 57,579 feet into the clouds. Eight hours later the couple landed. Jeannette had become the first woman to enter the earth's stratosphere.

Jeannette's life was very full during this time. In the 1930s she corresponded with scientists and mathematicians, such as Albert Einstein, Robert Andrews Millikan, W. F. G. Swann and A. W. Stevens. In 1937 she worked on the Pleides Project with her husband. Jean was professor of aeronautical engineering at the University of Minnesota and was busy trying to improve the equipment used for atmospheric research. He had already launched a cellophane balloon from the stadium at the University of Minnesota. The unmanned hydrogen-filled transparent cellophane balloon used the revolutionary adhesive-coated strips called Scotch tape and stayed in the air for ten hours.

Jean's idea for the *Pleides* was to build a large balloon made up of a cluster of smaller balloons. Getting funding from the Kiwanis Club of Rochester, Minnesota, the Piccards dove into this new project. They garnered help from many quarters: the Department of Mechanical Engineering of the University of Minnesota tested their materials, the aeronautical engineers gave sage advice, and the Commercial Gas Company of Minnesota furnished the hydrogen cylinders. The Pleides system used ninty-two latex balloons and a gondola of alclad sheets. The important task of supervising and coordinating the extensive ground crew required for such an endeavor fell to Jeannette. All the balloons had to be inflated separately and then had to be linked together. Jeannette was able to get her crew of 160 volunteers from the university and the Rochester area to master the task. The low-altitude test flight took off from Soldiers Field in Chicago on July 18, 1937.

Jeannette had not been able to go up with Jean for that flight, but she was not out of the skies yet. She was able to fly once again aboard the *Helios*. Similar to the *Pleides*, its main balloon was composed of nearly a hundred plastic balloons. This project allowed the Piccards to continue their upper-atmosphere research. Jeannette would set another record as she was carried in the sealed gondola to a height of 100,000 feet.

Jeannette continued her involvement with balloon research, but Jean was now hooked up with the Office of Naval Research, and the administration insisted that he fly only with navy pilots. Jeannette would not fly again, but she was undaunted in spirit and felt there was something new in the works for her. She had gone back to school and earned a PhD in education from the University of Minnesota in 1942. She worked for the Minnesota Office of Civil Defense in 1943 and became an aeronautical consultant for General Mills in 1947. Jeanette's early devotion to her church had never wavered, and now as president of the board of directors of the St. Paul's Episcopal Day School, she could devote some time to her religious interests.

During this time she kept meticulous care of the Piccard family papers. She collected and saved pertinent correspondence, memoranda, diaries, journals, logbooks, drafts of speeches, scrapbooks, photographs, news clippings, notes, and reports. She gave a collection of papers to the Library of Congress in 1969 and film footage of the 1934 stratospheric flight to the Motion Picture, Broadcasting, and Recorded Sound Division. She was named one of Minnesota's Women of Distinction in 1956.

Jean, professor emeritus of the University of Minnesota, died on his birthday, January 28, 1963. Jeannette called his death the result of a "psychologically induced heart attack." His brother, Auguste, had died the previous spring, and Jean had said that he didn't know how he could face a birthday without his twin. It was also in this year that Valentina Tereshkova entered outer space and broke Jeannette's record for women.

Jeannette's next project saw her as consultant to the director of NASA's Manned Spacecraft Center, now the Johnson Space Center. She served from 1964, just after Jean's death, until 1970.

She received a Certificate of Honor from the National Aeronautics Association in 1966 and the Outstanding Achievement Award from the University of Minnesota in 1968.

The new decade brought a wonderful opportunity for Jeannette, one she had been waiting for nearly all her life. It was 1972, and as she walked the tree-shaded Chelsea campus, she could hardly believe she was at long last a student at the General Theological Seminary. It had been fifty-four years since she had first planned to attend the seminary upon her graduation from Bryn Mawr way back in 1918. Because of her vast experience in church matters and the amount of reading she had done on the subject over the years, it took 77-year-old Jeannette only one year to complete her studies at the seminary instead of the three usually required to qualify for the priesthood.

But the road ahead was not a smooth one. The Episcopal Church had not legally accepted women into the priesthood, although there were many who wanted to change the law. Ten other women were eligible for ordination, and some felt the time was right to make a move. When three bishops agreed to perform the ceremony, the stage was set for a history-making event.

The eleven women arrived at the Church of the Advocate on the feast of Saints Martha and Mary of Bethany. It was July 29, 1974, a humid Monday morning in the middle of summer. The huge Gothic Revival church in the heart of North Philadelphia could hold more than 2,000 people. There was plenty of opposition and much concern that rioting, arson, or other tactics would stop the ceremony. By 11:00 A.M. the church was packed; the press and TV cameras were there too. In his opening remarks the rector likened the event to the birth of a baby by saying, "The church says it's an inconvenient time to have a birth, but the baby comes when its time is here." With that the ceremony began. The sermon of the day spoke of justice delayed as justice denied. When the appointed time came for objections, a long line of clergy formed. All had their say, then the bishop read a simple statement of intent to continue with the ordinations. All the women took their vows together in a service that lasted three hours—due to both the cheering and the protesting. Jeannette could count about a hundred priests joining in for the laying on of hands amid the continuous flashing of cameras. By the end of the ceremony, those opposed had left. Jeannette was astounded at the outpouring of love and support of those who remained to greet the daring "irregularly" ordained first women priests of the Episcopal Church.

On August 15 the House of Bishops convened an emergency meeting to denounce the ordinations. The three ordaining bishops were censured and two priests who had invited the women to celebrate the Eucharist in their parishes were put on ecclesiastical trial. Attempts were made to prevent the women from their priestly ministry, but the women would not back down. On October 27, 1974, three months after their Philadelphia ceremony, three of the women celebrated their first Episcopal Eucharist service at the Riverside Church in New York City—Jeannette was one of them. She boldly celebrated the service looking out over the faithful of the huge Gothic church that covered two city blocks on the Upper West Side of New York City. It was from this church, modeled after the thirteenth-century Chartres Cathedral in France, that Martin Luther King Jr. had delivered his now-famous anti-Vietnam speech. She was proud to be among such company.

Women's struggle for ordination rites in the Episcopal Church had begun in the 1850s and had lasted 125 years. Jeannette had been preparing to enter the priesthood for sixty of those years. On September 16, 1976, the General Convention of the Episcopal Church, ironically meeting in Minneapolis, the home of Rev. Jeannette Piccard, voted to approve women's ordination to the priesthood, and the eleven women were finally accepted legally.

One of the highlights of Jeannette's religious life was that she was asked to give the invocation in the Minnesota House of Representatives in 1974.

Jeannette served as deacon of Saint Phillip's of Saint Paul, Minnesota, and then as co-priest from 1975 to 1977. She became an honorary canon in 1981, living her passion until the end. She died of cancer on May 17, 1981, at the Masonic Memorial Hospital in Minneapolis.

Jean and Jeannette were inducted into the International Space Hall of Fame in Alamogordo, New Mexico in 1998 in recognition of their lifetime achievements in aeronautics. Their *Century of Progress* gondola is on display at the Chicago Museum of Science and Industry. Jeannette was active in the National Organization of Women (NOW), the League of Women Voters, and the AAUW. Jeannette lived to see her grandchildren and her great-grandchildren. She and Jean were part of a large family of space and sea explorers, but perhaps she would have been most proud of her granddaughter, Kathryn Ann Piccard, who was also ordained as an Episcopal priest.

BIBLIOGRAPHY

About Carrie Chapman Catt. Accessed July 10, 2003, from www.catt.org/ ccabout.html.

Adams, Susan. "Flashbacks." Forbes, vol. 167, January 16, 2001, 32.

"Americans Still Remember Australian Polio Pioneer." *Australian Nursing Journal,* vol. 7, April 2000, 8.

Annis, Diana Kenney. *American National Biography Online: Elizabeth Kenny.* Accessed April 8, 2002, from www.anb.org.

Archabal, Nina Marchetti. *Frances Densmore: Pioneer in the Study of American Indian Music.* Accessed August 30, 2001, from news.mpr.org/features/ 199702/01_smiths_densmore/docs/archabal/shtml.

Aritage, Katie. *Langston Hughes' Lawrence.* Accessed June 5, 2003, from www.ci.lawrence.ks.us/langston.

Beell, Thomas. "Journalism, Home Economics Good Combination for '28 Grad." Accessed June 17, 2003, from www.jlmc.iastate.edu.

Berman, Hyman. *Jews in Minnesota.* St. Paul: Minnesota Historical Society, 2001.

Biltmore Hotel. Accessed May 30, 2003, from www.dacamera.org/ Concerts/mnf/budapest.htm.

Biography of Elizabeth Kenny. Accessed January 24, 2003, from www.mnhs.org/library/findaids/00201.html.

Blau, Eleanor. "Balloonist's Widow, 77, Joins Seminary." *New York Times Biographical Edition,* October 1972, vol. 12.

Breining, Greg. *Minnesota.* Oakland CA: Compass American Guides, 1997.

BIBLIOGRAPHY

Caldwell, Matthew. Sermon, Church of the Good Shepherd, July 28, 2002.

Carney, Mary Vance. *Minnesota: The Star of the North*. Chicago: D.C. Heath & Co., Publishers, 1918.

Chinese Immigration to Minnesota. Accessed July 16, 2002, from www.making connections.state.mn.

Chinese Laundry. Accessed July 16, 2002, from www.askasia.org/frclasrm/ readings.

A Chronology of Events Concerning Women in Holy Orders. Women's Ministries. Accessed June 22, 2003, from www.episcopalchurch.org.

"City Seeks Funding to Rehab Historic Statue." *American City & County*, May 2000, 62.

Contemporary Authors Online. Accessed January 27, 2003 from www.galenet.com.

Contemporary Authors Online. Wanda (Hazel) Gag. Accessed January 26, 2002, from web6.infotrac.galegroup.com.

Crouch, Tom. *The Eagle Aloft*. Washington, DC: Smithsonian Institution Press, 1983.

Curtis, Dorothy E. "Elizabeth Kenny Unlocks the Puzzle of Polio." *Child Life*, vol. 81, January/February 2002, 20–24.

"Cuthbert Calculus." *Tintin and Friends*. Accessed June 16, 2003, from rbhatta.freeyellow.com/page6.html.

Dashefsky, Arnold, and Howard M. Shipiro. *Ethnic Identification among American Jews*. Lexington, MA: D.C. Heath and Company, 1974.

Davis-Kay, Jennifer. *The Betsy-Tacy Society Home Page*. Accessed June 22, 2003, from www.betsy-tacysociety.org.

DuSablon, Mary Anna. *American National Biography Online: Marjorie Child Husted*. Accessed February 18, 2002, from www.anb.org/articles/ 20/20-01577.html.

BIBLIOGRAPHY

Episode 854 — TV Tome. Accessed January 26, 2003, from www
.tvtome.com.

Glotzbach, G. L. "Wanda Gag Collection Open for Research." *Horn Book Magazine,* January 1992, 122.

General Mills Flour: Our Heritage. Accessed June19, 2003, from www
.generalmills.com.

Governor's Interracial Commission. *The Oriental in Minnesota.* St. Paul: State of Minnesota, 1949.

Guthrey, Molly. "Loud and Clear." *St. Paul Pioneer Press,* March 20
1999, D1.

Gutis, Philip S. "Marjorie Husted Dead as 94; Helped Create Betty Crocker." *New York Times,* December 12, 1986, 19.

Hamernick, Joseph M., S.J. "Blanche Yurka." *Best Sellers,* July 15, 1970,
166.

Harriet Island Regional Park. Accessed May 27, 2003, from nps.gov/
miss/maps/model/harriet.html.

High Flier Jeannette Piccard. Accessed June 16, 2003, from www.write
tools.com/women/stories/piccard_jeanette.html.

The Historic Pantages Theatre. Accessed June 5, 2003, from www.hennepin
theatredistrict.com.

History of First Baptist Church. Accessed May 27, 2003, from www
.firstbaptiststpaul.org/history.html.

The History of Lawrence. Accessed June 5, 2003, from www.visit
lawrence.com.

Hoffert, Sylvia. "Jane Grey Swisshelm and the Negotiation of Gender Roles on the Minnesota Frontier." *Frontiers,* vol. 18, no. 3, 1997, 17–40.

BIBLIOGRAPHY

Holland, Henry. *Dr. Henry Writes about Sister Kenny: Polio Pioneer.* Accessed April 12, 2002, from www.ott.zynet.co.uk/polio/lincolnshire/library/drhenry/srkenny.html.

Holmquist, June Drenning, ed. *They Chose Minnesota.* St. Paul, Minnesota: Minnesota Historical Society Press, 1981.

Jaakkola, Terry, and Julia Lambert Frericks. *Shadows Illuminated: Women in a Rural Culture.* St. Cloud, Minnesota: Stearns County Historical Society, 1996.

Juergens, Ann. "Lena Olive Smith: A Minnesota Civil Rights Pioneer." *William Mitchell Law Review,* 28, 2001, 397.

Keillor, Elaine. *American National Biography Online: Densmore, Frances Theresa.* Accessed February 18, 2002, from www.anb.org.

Kinnell, Susan K., ed. *People in History: An Index to U.S. and Canadian Biographies in History Journals and Dissertations.* Santa Barbara, CA: ABC-CLIO, 1988.

Kron, Einar E. *A Chautauqua Summer.* Accessed June 5, 2003, from www.lib,uiowa.edu/spec-coll.

Marquardt, Hagelstein. "Art on the Political Front in America." *Art Journal,* Spring 1993, 72–82.

Mason, Sarah Refo. "Liang May Seen and the Early Chinese Community in Minneapolis." *Minnesota History.* Spring 1995, 223–33.

McMein, Neysa. *Women in American History.* Accessed June 6, 2003, from www.eb.com/women/articles/McMein-Neysa.html.

Medicine. Accessed March 20, 2002, from www.mpls.lib.mn.us/history/rs3.asp.

Meier, Peg. "Childbirth Pioneer." *Star Tribune: Newspaper of the Twin Cities.* March, 14, 1999, 1E.

"Minneapolis-Saint Paul." *Encyclopedia Judaica,* CD-ROM, 2003 edition.

BIBLIOGRAPHY

Minnesota Author Biographies Project. "Frances Densmore." Accessed August 30, 2001, from http://people.mnhs.org/authors/index.cfm.

Minnesota Historical Society. "Harriet Bishop." Accessed January 22, 2002, from www.mnhs.org/places/historycenter/programs/theater/harriet.html.

————. *Maud Hart Lovelace.* Accessed January 22, 2002, from www.mnhs.org.

————. Ripley Memorial Foundation. Accessed March 21, 2002, from www.mnhs.org.

"Mrs. Brin is Dead: Led Jewish Group." *New York Times,* Sepember 7, 1961, ObitB5.

1936 Academy Awards. Accessed January 26, 2003, from www.info please.com/ipa.

Ortakales, Denise. *Women's Children's Book Illustrators: Wanda Hazel Gag.* Accessed May 24, 2002, from www.ortakales.com/illustrators/Gag.html.

Oscars and Other Awards. Accessed May 30, 2003, from www.oscars .org/academy awards/awards/index.html

Perri, Klass. "Betsy, Tacy, and Tib." *Victoria,* April 1998, 120–23.

Peschel, Bill. *American National Biography Online: Gag Wanda.* Accessed April 8, 2002, from www.anb.org/articles/16/16-0063.html.

Plaut, Gunther W. *The Jews in Minnesota.* New York: American Jewish Historical Society, 1959.

Quindlen, Anna. "Betsy Ray, Feminist Icon." *School Library Journal,* November 1993, 26–32.

"The Real Betsy Ray." *School Library Journal,* January 1996, 40.

Rothe, Anna, ed. "Marjorie Child Husted." *Current Biography.* New York: The H. W. Wilson Company, 1949, 286.

Rudavsky, Shari. *American National Biography Online: Martha George Ripley.* Accessed Febuary 2002, from www.anb.org/articles/12/ 12-01605.html.

Salk, Jonas, M.D. Accessed June 12, 2003, from www.achievement.org.

The Salk Vaccine. Accessed June 12, 2003, from www.geocities.com/harpub/ salkvaccine.

Sass, Edmund. *Remembering Polio: A Ghost from Summers Past.* Accessed June 12, 2003, from www.employees.csbsju.edu.

Schloff, Linda Mack. *And Prairie Dogs Weren't Kosher: Jewish Women in the Upper Midwest since 1855.* St. Paul: Minnesota Historical Society Press, 1966.

Sheehy, Colleen. *Wanda Gag Essay.* Accessed May 24, 2002, from www.hudson.acad.umn.edu/G%87g/Essay.html.

Siegel, Reva B. "Home as Work: The First Women's Rights Claims concerning Wives' Household Labor, 1850–1880." *Yale Law Journal,* vol. 103, no. 5, 1994, 1073–1217.

Sister Elizabeth Kenny—"A Brief History." Accessed April 12, 2002, from www.sisterkenny.org.au/history.htm.

Smith, John D., Esq. Panton. Accessed May 27, 2003, from www.newsarch.rootsweb.com.

Solberg, Winton U. "Martha G. Ripley: Pioneer Doctor and Social Reformer." *Minnesota History,* vol. 39, 1964, 1–17.

Sommerdorf, Norma. "Harriet E. Bishop, a Doer and a Mover." *Minnesota History,* Fall 1997, 320–23.

Sorenson, Paul. *Inventing Tomorrow. Up, Up, and Away.* Accessed June 7, 2003, from www.itdean.umn.edu/inventing/98fall/retrospect.html.

Stekel, Peter. *Don Piccard—50 Years of Ballooning Memories.* Accessed June 7, 2003, from www.balloonlife.com/publications/balloon_life/ 9707/piccard.htm.

BIBLIOGRAPHY

Stuhler, Barbara. *Women of Minnesota: Selected Biographical Essays.* St. Paul: Minnesota Historical Press, 1998.

———— and Gretchen Kreuter, eds. *Women of Minnesota: Selected Biographical Essays.* St. Paul: Minnesota Historical Society Press, 1977.

Suggs, Henry Lewis. *The Black Press in the Middle West, 1865–1985.* Westport, CT: Greenwood Press, 1996.

Swisshelm, Jane Grey. *Half a Century.* Chicago: Jansen, McClurg and Company, 1880.

Truman Presidential Museum and Library. Accessed July 10, 2003, from www.trumanlibrary.org.

Vannote, Vance. *Women of White Earth.* Minneapolis: University of Minnesota Press, 1999.

Vaz, Kim Marie. *Black Women in America.* Thousand Oaks, CA: Sage Publications, 1995.

A Visit to the Five Hometown Counties of Overseas Chinese. Accessed July 17, 2002, from www.gdnet.gd.cei.gov.cn/gdnnet/todaygd/travel/ll_html_e.htm.

Waggoner, Walter. "Rev. Jeannette Piccard Dies at 86; Scientist Entered Seminary in '70." *New York Times,* May 19, 1981, 18.

Wanda Gag: Artist and Author. Accessed May 24, 2002, from www.new ulmtel.net/history/stories/wandagag.html.

Wanda Gag. Minnesota Author Biographies Project. Accessed April 11, 2002, from www.people.mnhs.org/authors.

Wanda Gag Papers. Accessed May 24, 2002, from www.avatar.lib.usm .edu/~degrum/finaids/gag.htm.

Washburn-Crosby Cooking: Gold Medal/General Mills/Betty Crocker Cookbooks. Accessed June 19, 2003, from www.friktech.com.

BIBLIOGRAPHY

WCCO Radio. WCCO Radio. Accessed June 19, 2003, from www.ci .coon-rapids.mn.us.

Wingerd, Mary Lethert. *Claiming the City: Politics, Faith, and the Power of Place in St. Paul.* Ithaca, NY: Cornell University Press, 2001.

Women in American History: Majorie Child Husted. Accessed June 6, 2003, from www.eb.com/women/articles/Husted_Marjorie.html.

"The Wonder Down Under." *Jack & Jill,* vol. 63, June 2001, 32–34.

World's Columbian Exposition. *The Legacy of the Fair.* Accessed October 18, 2001, from xroads.virginia.edu/~MA96/WCE/legacy.html.

Yanisch, Barbara Mader. *"Maud Hart Lovelace as 'Betsy Ray.'"* Accessed June 22, 2003, from www.geocities.com/Paris/Lights/4859/ maudasbetsy.html.

Yurka, Blanche. *Bohemian Girl: Blanche Yurka's Theatrical Life.* Athens: Ohio University Press, 1970.

ℐNDEX

About the Author

Bonnye Stuart is a college professor and writer who taught in the mass communications department at St. Cloud State University for five years. Bonnye is a Minnesotan on her father's side, and although she spent her growing up years in New Orleans, she always felt very connected to her Minnesota roots—even if the mittens and ear muffs her Minnesota grandmother sent every Christmas seemed quite an oddity. Her publishing credits include two plays and several articles.